Sisters

EDITED BY SARAH ARAK

Sisters
Copyright © 2006, Silverback Books, Inc.

All rights reserved. No part of this book may be used or reproduced in any manner whatsoever without prior written permission of the publisher.

Photographs courtesy of Jupiterimages.
Used with permission. All rights reserved.

Cover design by Richard Garnas
Interior design and production by Patty Holden

ISBN: 1-59637-066-1

Printed and bound in China

Introduction

In early childhood, sisters are often each other's first real friends—allies in discovery, mischief, learning and play. During adolescence, once-close sisters may temporarily weaken their ties as they exert their individuality and independence. But the bond of sisterhood often becomes strongest in adulthood, when the pressures of family life, career and motherhood are strongest. Just as they shared toys and clothes as children, sisters generally want to share their adult struggles and triumphs with each other.

The bittersweet bond between sisters is the most enduring relationship most women have in their lifetimes—longer even than the mother/child or husband/wife relationship. Sisters know each other better than perhaps anyone else in the world, and this knowledge forges an unbreakable link between them, one that can span even the greatest geographical and emotional distances.

While this bond may wax and wane over time, a woman's lifetime quest for personal identity is undeniably interwoven with that of her sister's. Their paths through life may diverge widely at times, but it is the natural tendency of sisters to converge, from time to time, and walk side by side.

SISTERHOOD IS PROBABLY THE MOST

COMPETITIVE RELATIONSHIP WITHIN THE FAMILY,

BUT ONCE THE SISTERS ARE GROWN,

IT BECOMES THE STRONGEST.

—Margaret Mead

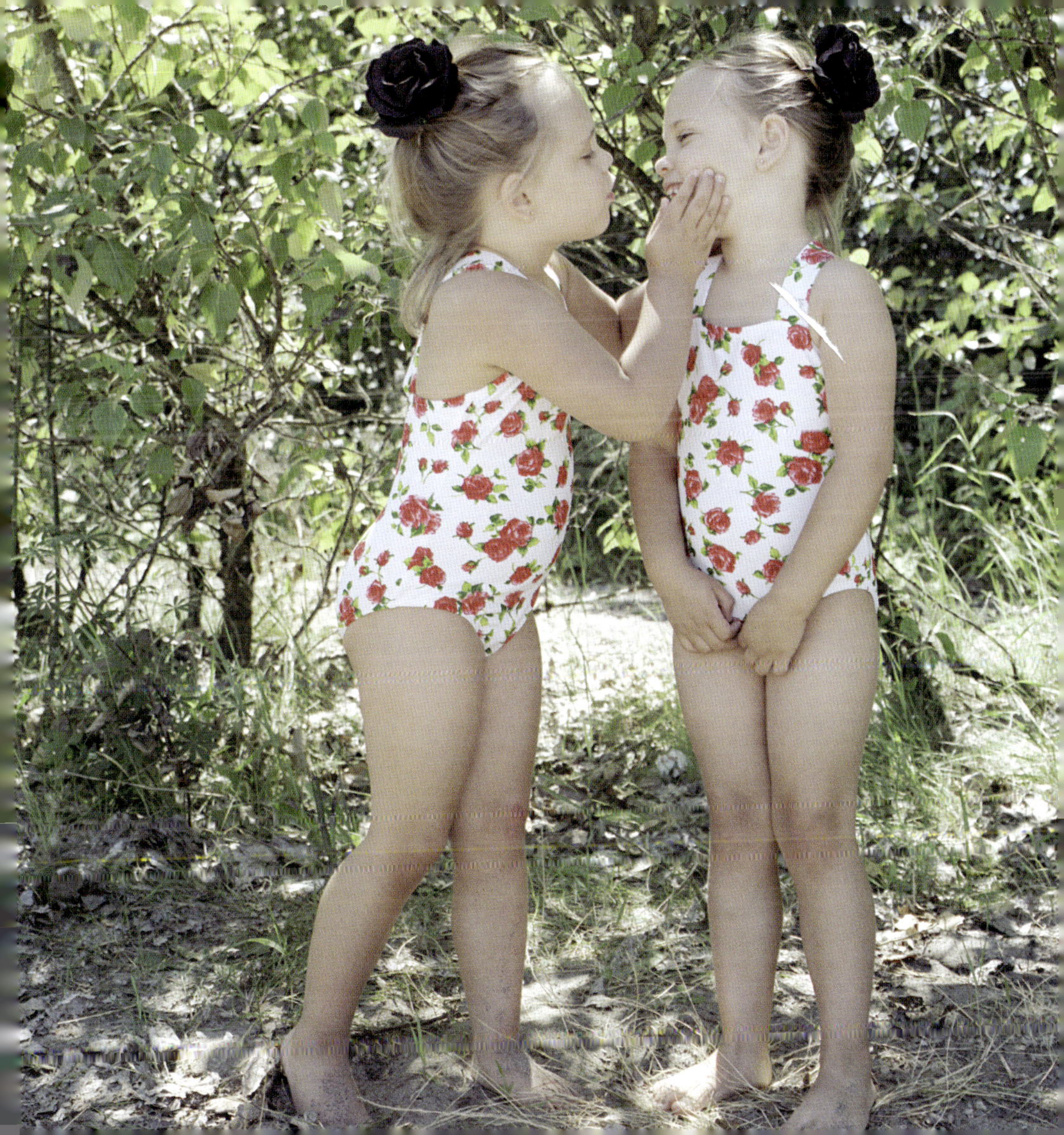

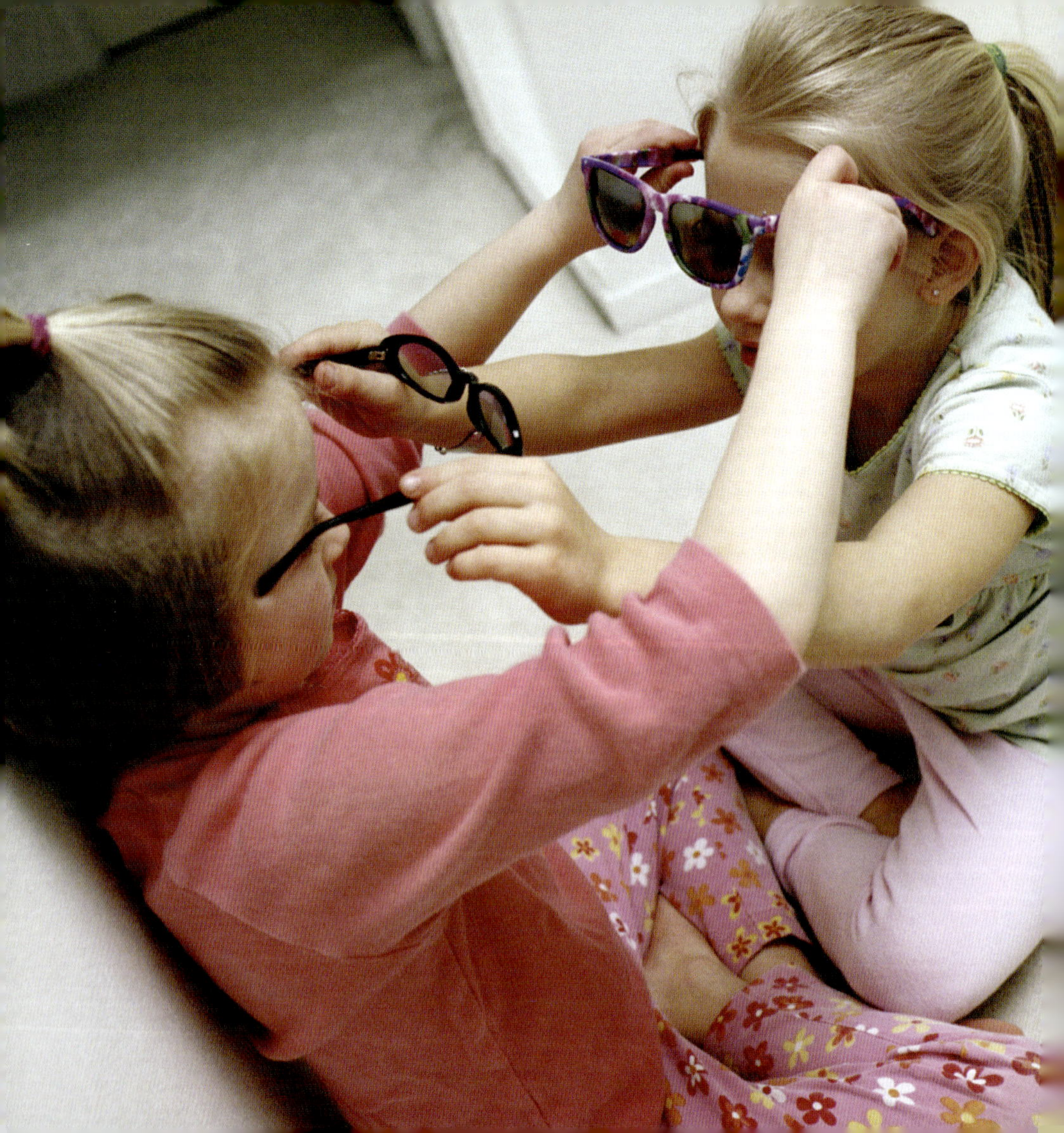

A SISTER IS A LITTLE BIT OF

CHILDHOOD THAT CAN NEVER BE LOST.

—Marion C. Garretty

To the outside world, we all grow old.

But not to sisters. We know each other as

we always were. We know each other's hearts.

We share private family jokes. We remember

family feuds and secrets, family griefs and joys.

We live outside the touch of time.

—Clara Ortega

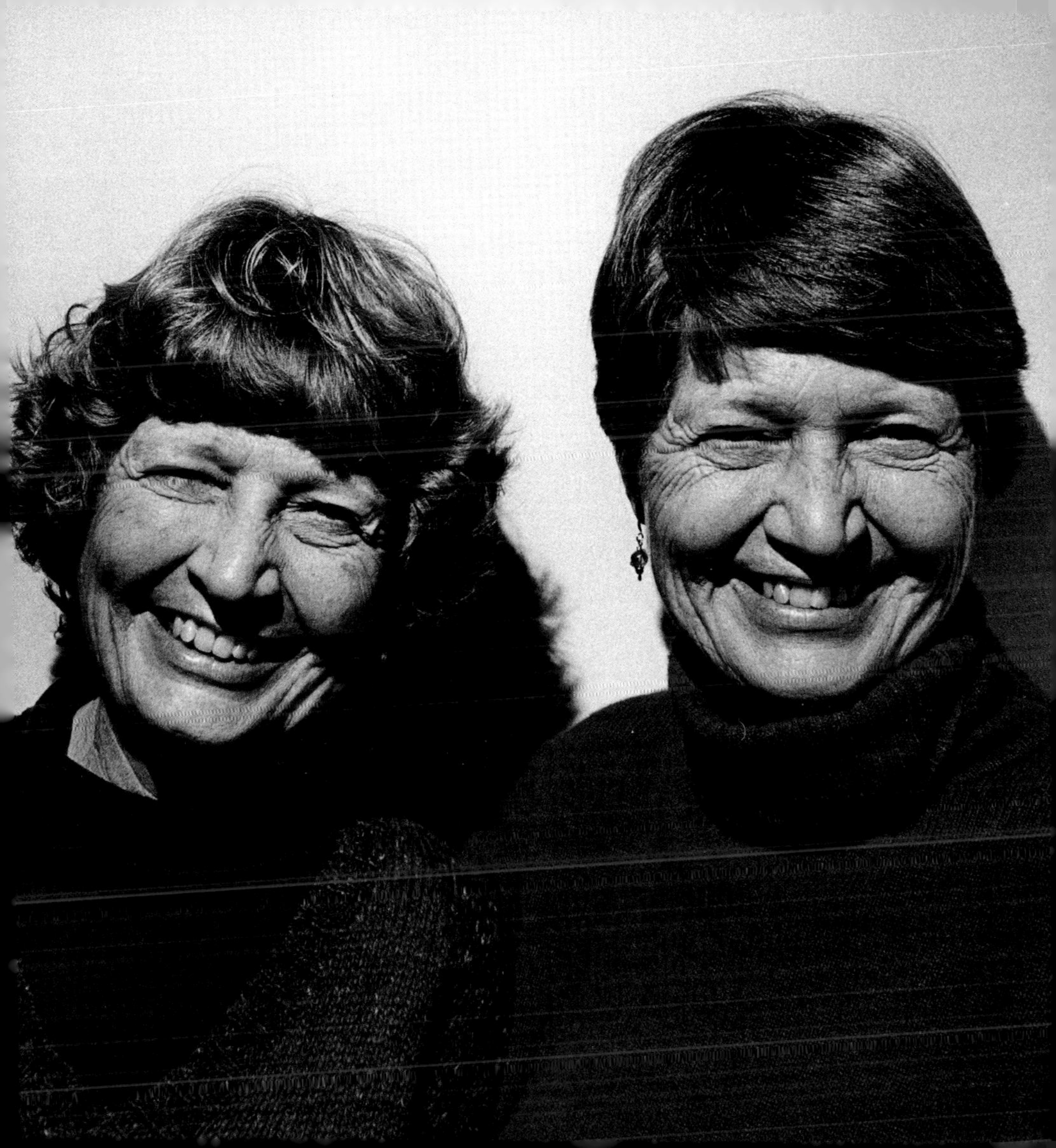

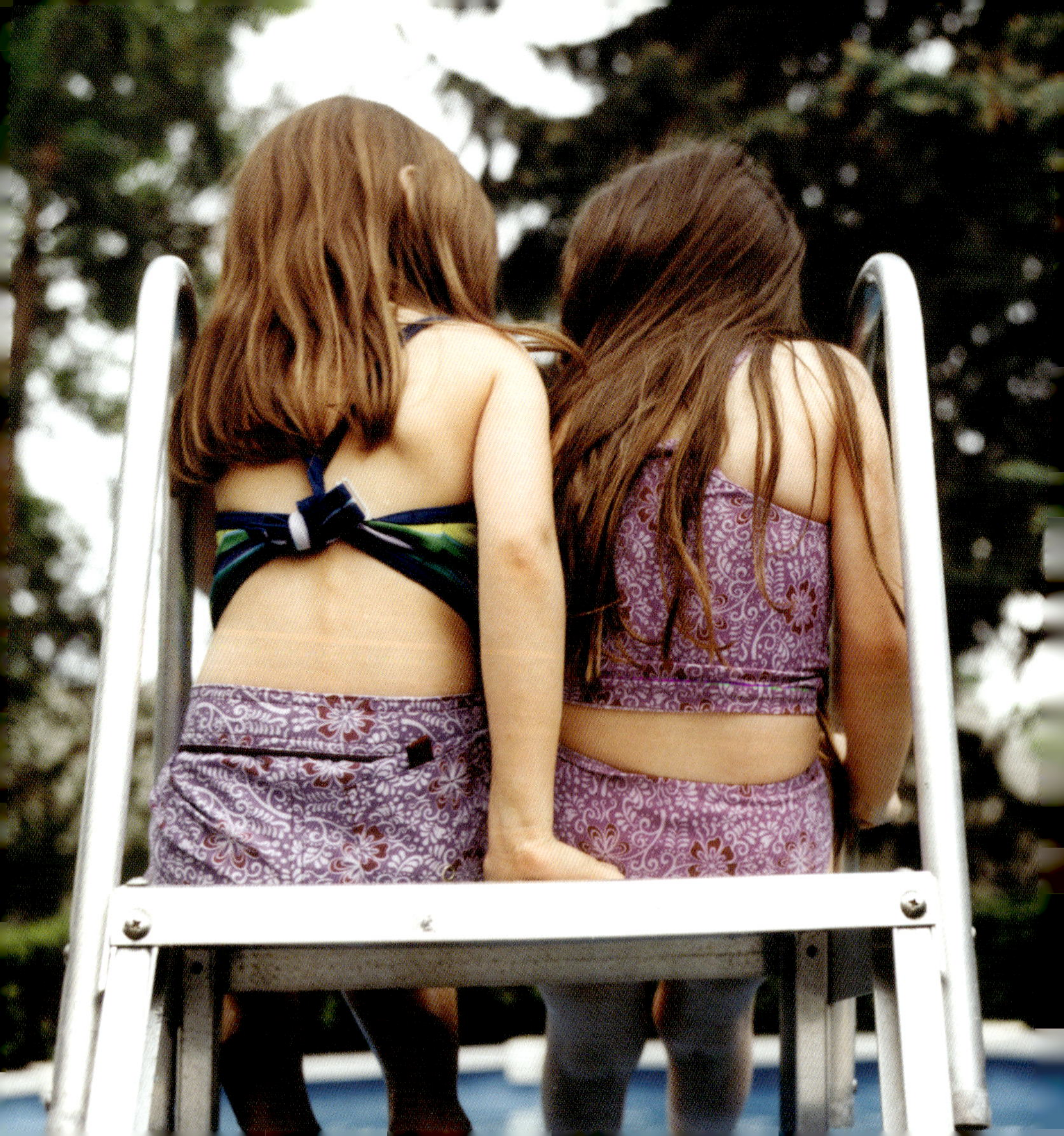

I ALWAYS LIKE TO WIN. BUT I'M THE BIG SISTER.

I WANT TO MAKE SURE SHE HAS EVERYTHING,

EVEN IF I DON'T HAVE ANYTHING.

— Venus Williams

A PERFECT SISTER I AM NOT, BUT

THANKFUL FOR THE ONE I'VE GOT.

—Author Unknown

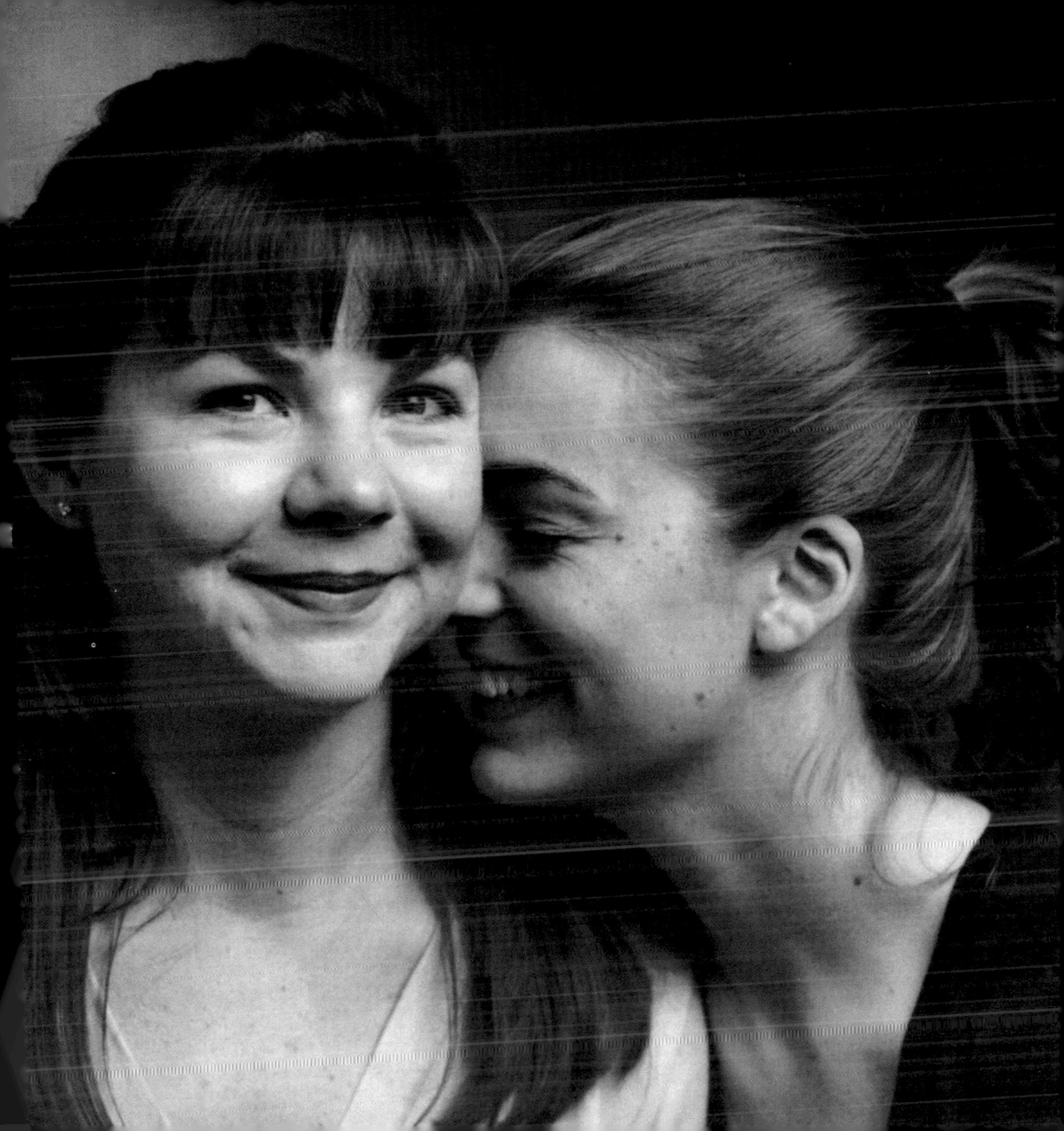

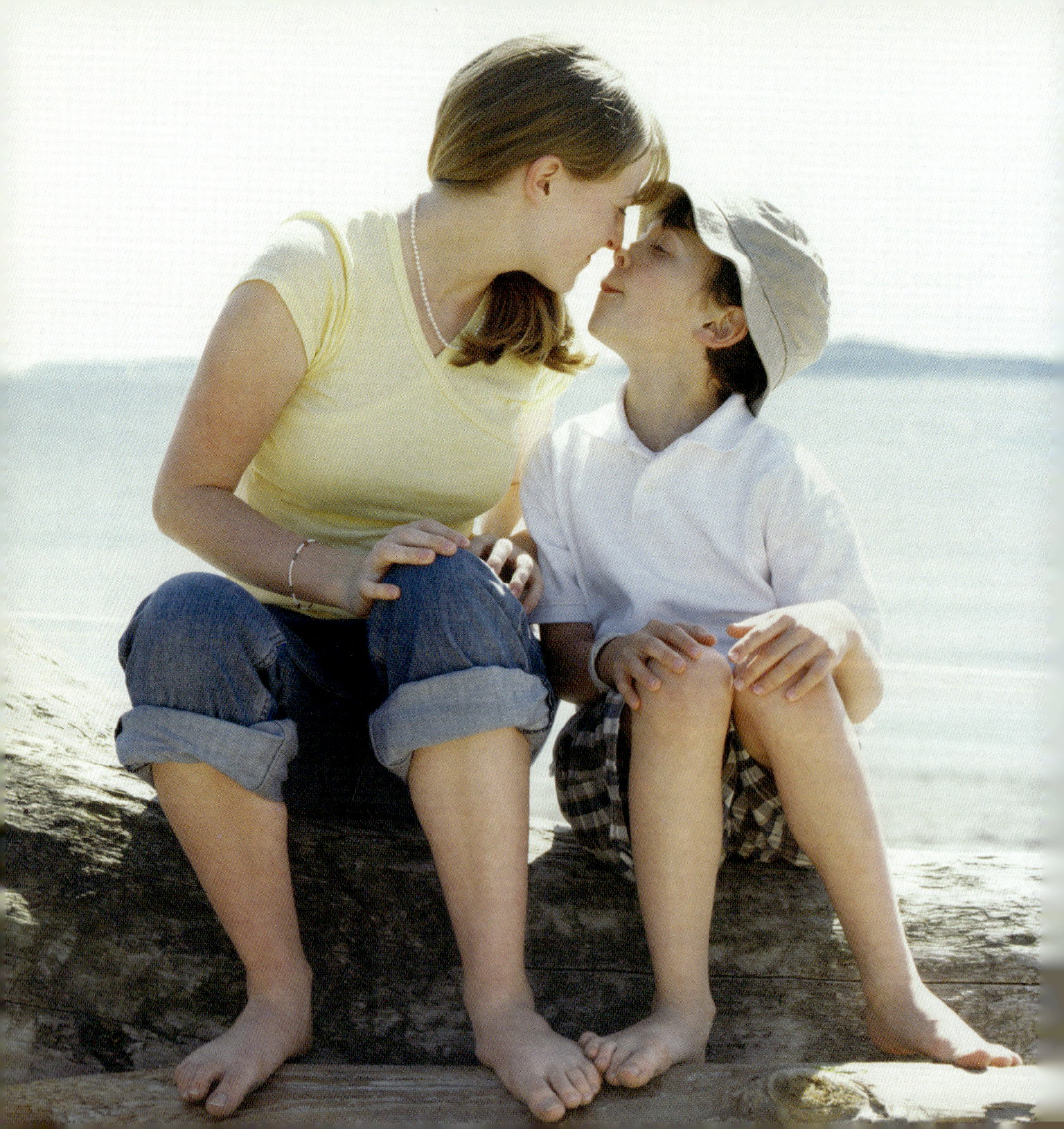

Having a sister is like having a best friend you can't get rid of. You know whatever you do, they'll still be there.

—Amy Li

It was nice growing up with someone

like you—someone to lean on,

someone to count on...someone to tell on!

—Author Unknown

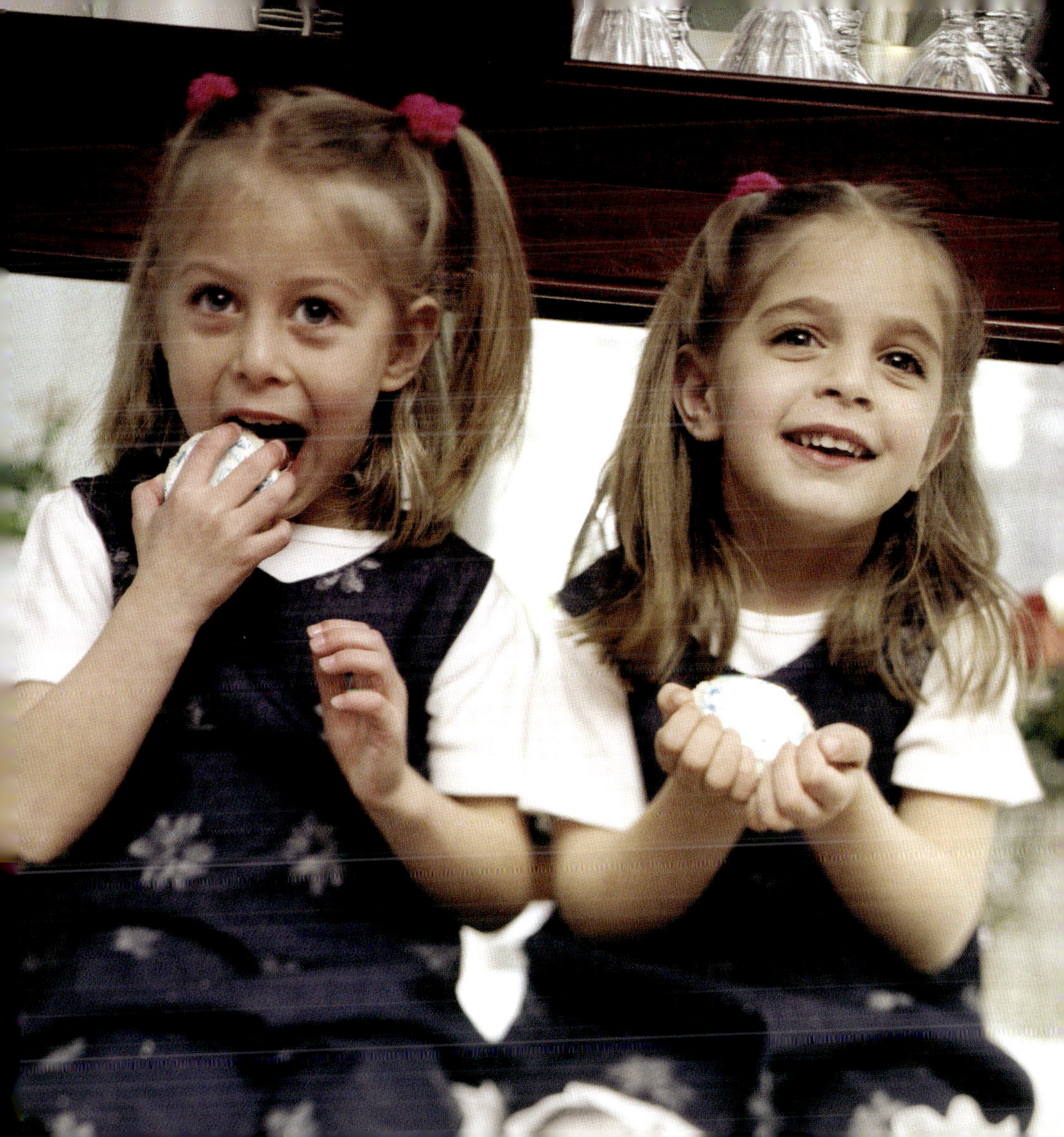

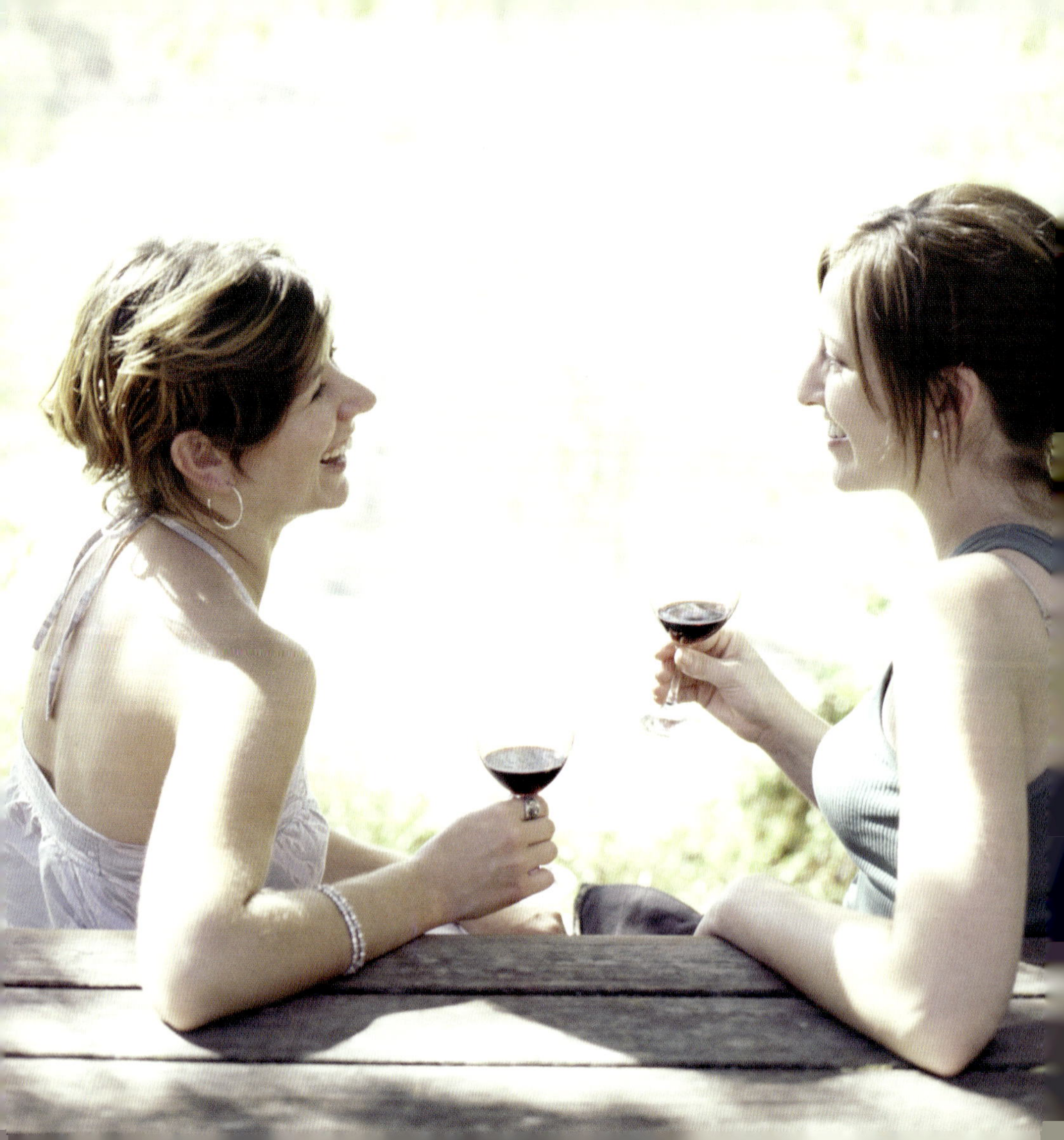

A SISTER SMILES WHEN ONE TELLS ONE'S

STORIES—FOR SHE KNOWS WHERE THE

DECORATION HAS BEEN ADDED.

— Chris Montaigne

A SISTER IS A GIFT TO THE HEART,

A FRIEND TO THE SPIRIT, A GOLDEN THREAD

TO THE MEANING OF LIFE.

—Isadora James

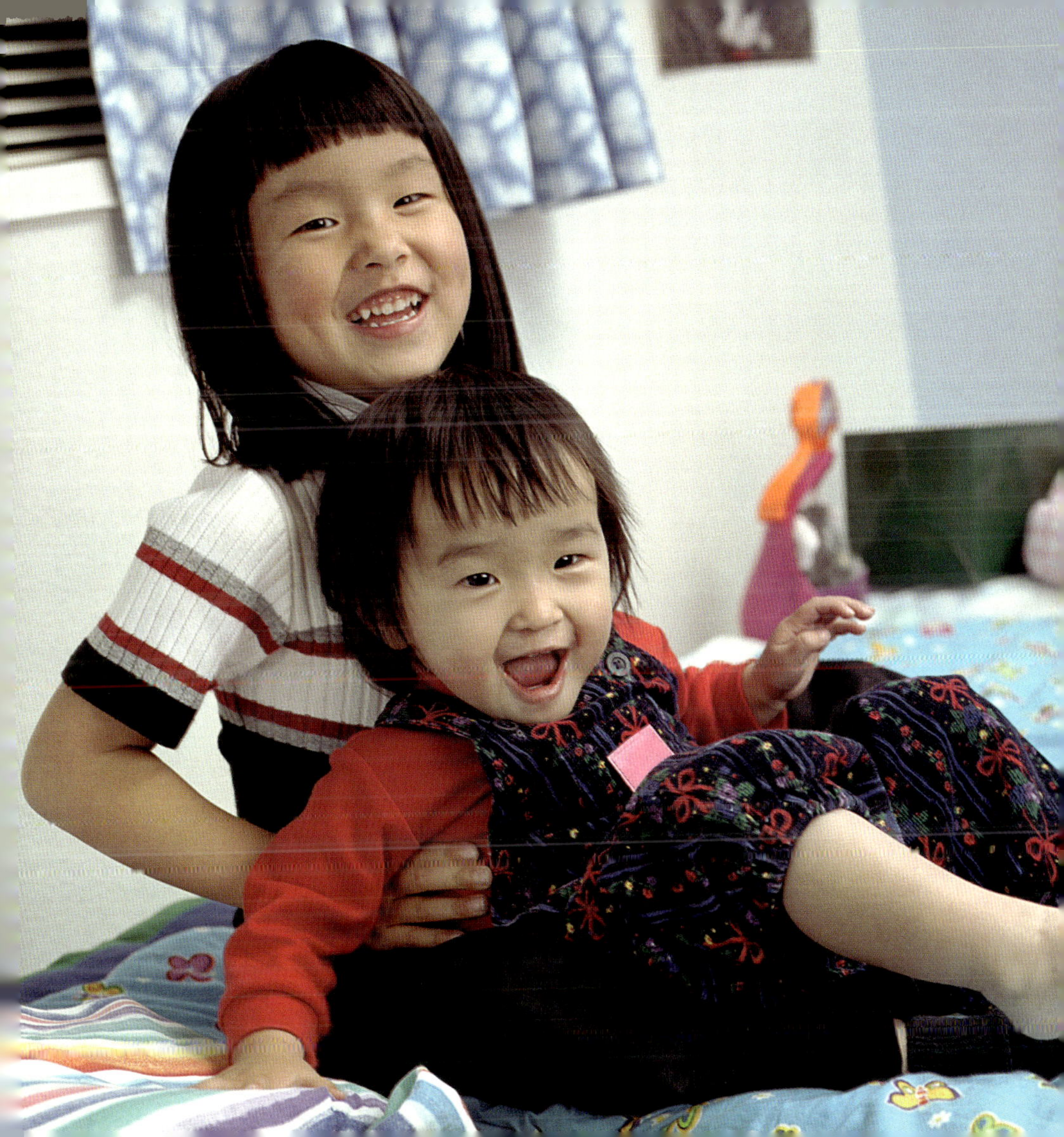

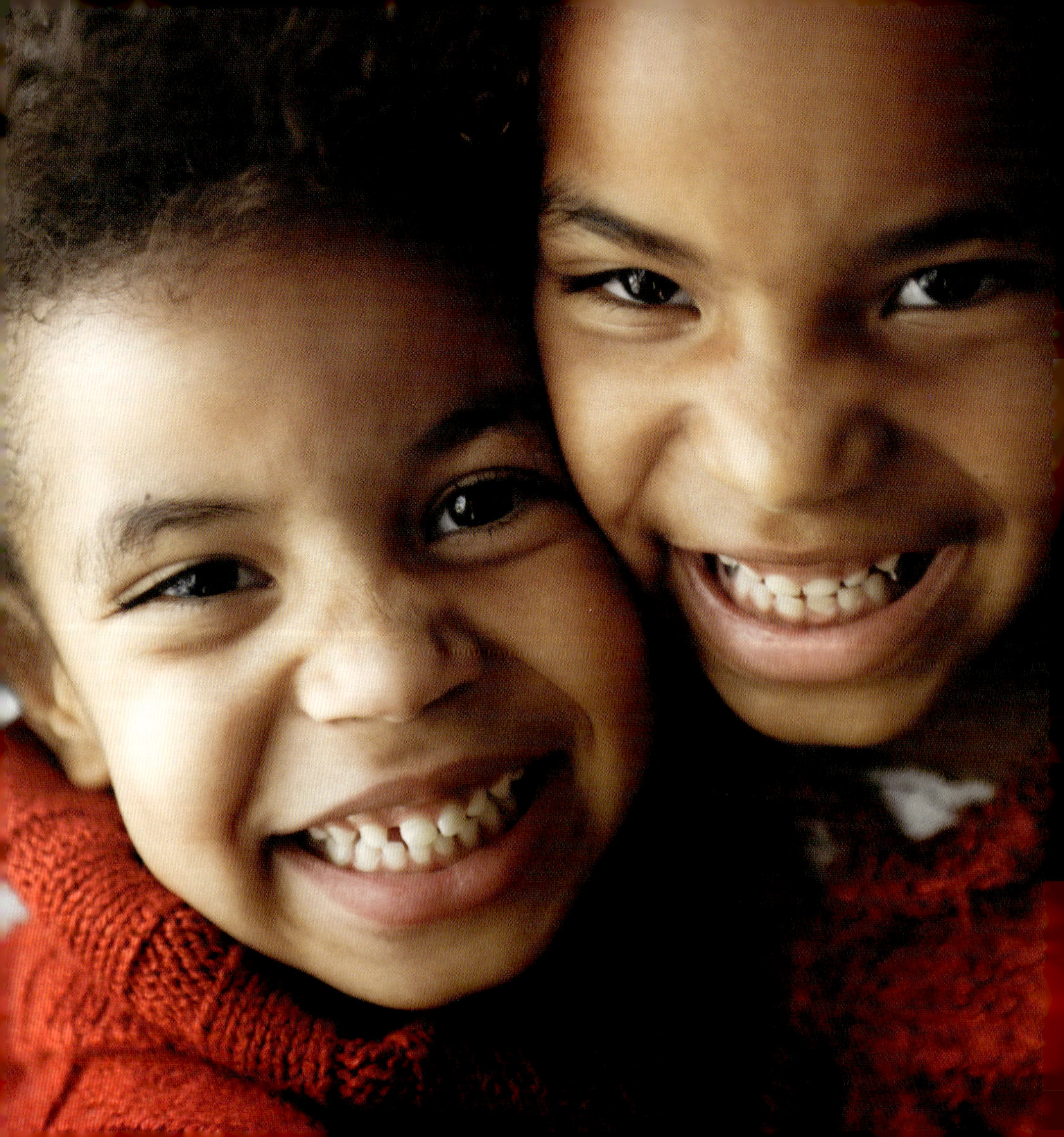

What's the use of good of news if you

haven't a sister to share it with?

—Jenny DeVries

Sisters annoy, interfere, criticize.

Indulge in monumental sulks, in huffs,

in snide remarks. Borrow. Break. Monopolize

the bathroom. Are always underfoot. But if

catastrophe should strike, sisters are there.

Defending you against all comers.

— Pam Brown

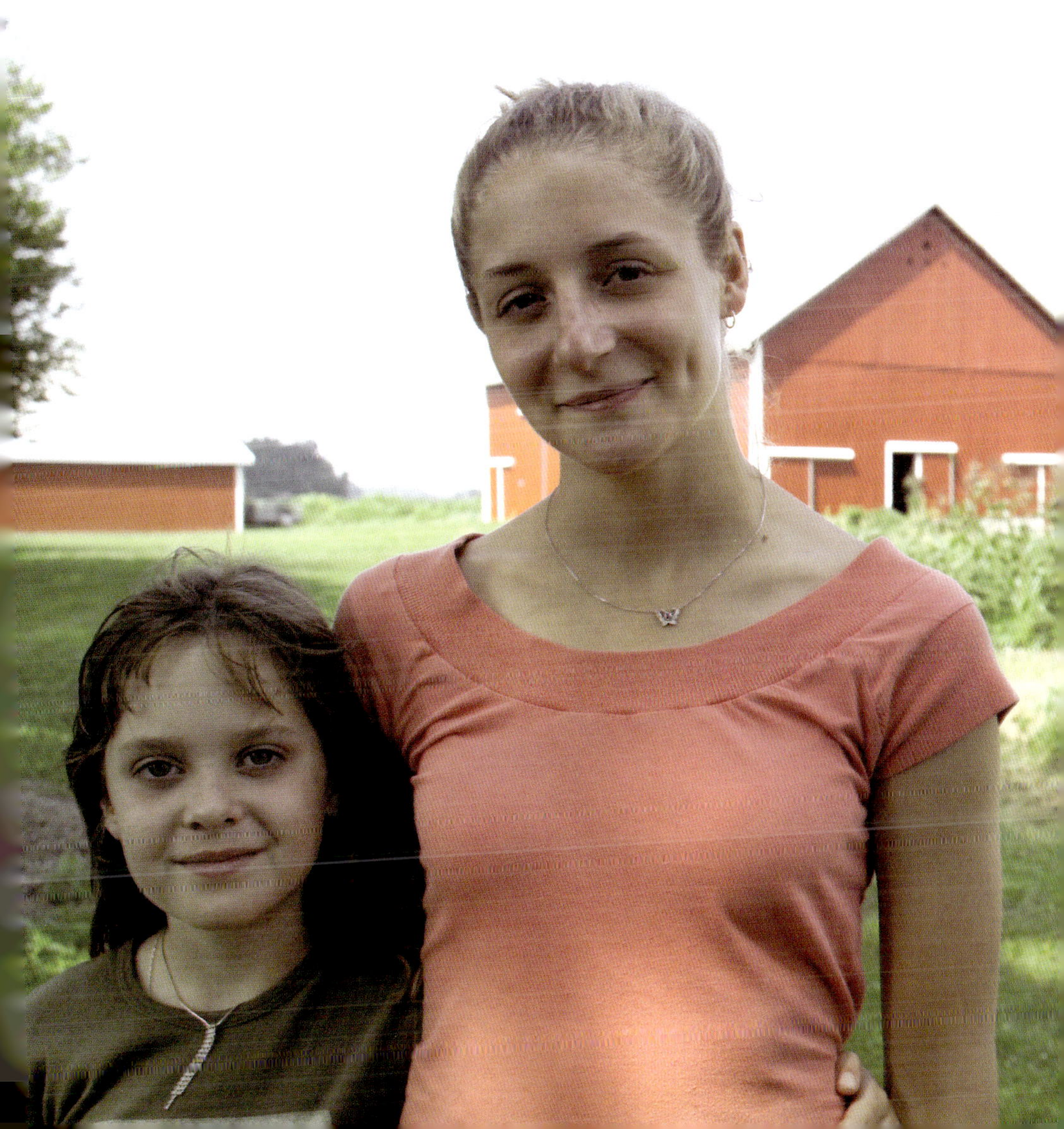

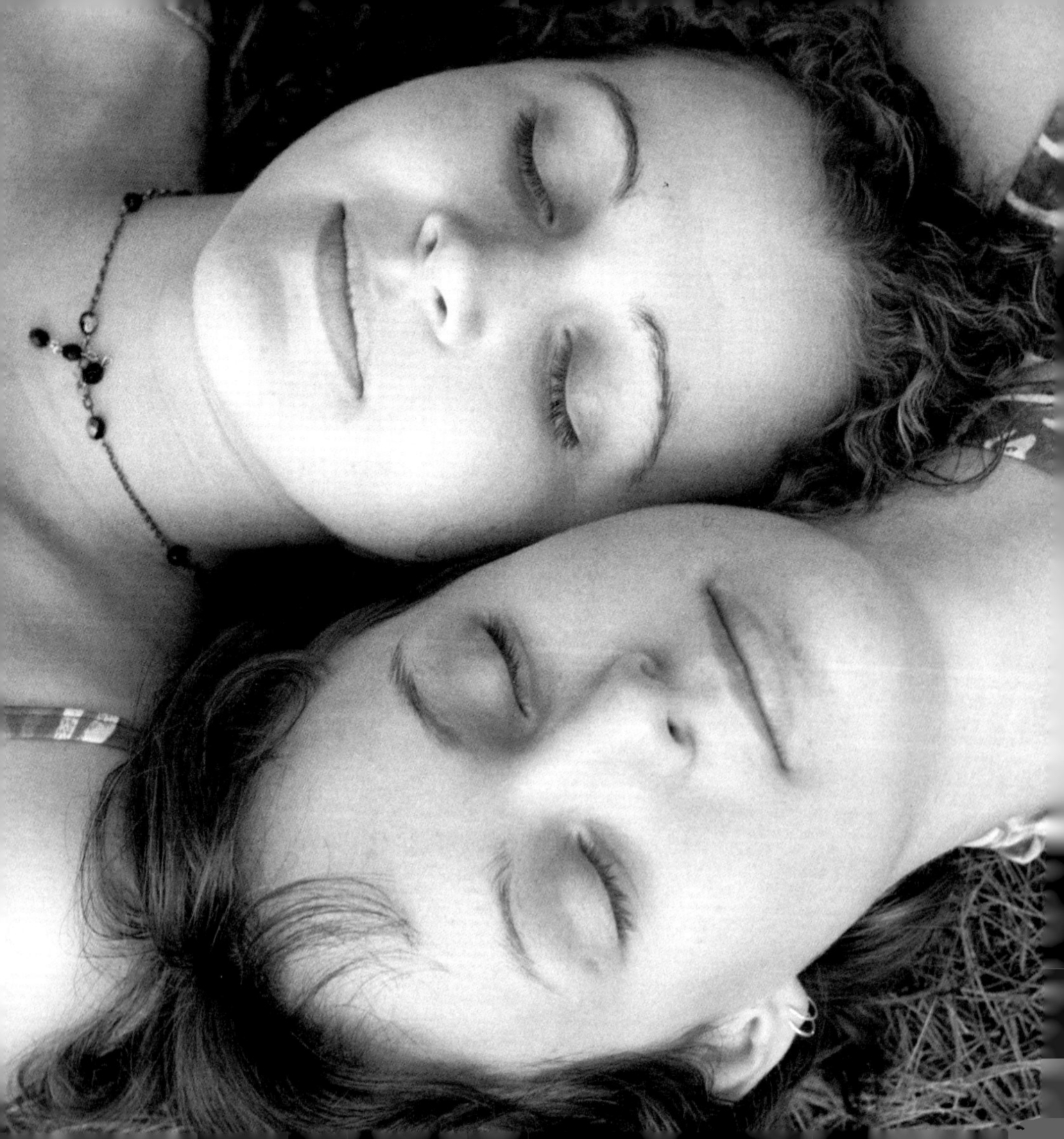

That beautiful sister of mine was an overwhelming and volatile mixture. One had the feeling that she'd been shot from a canon and showered her sparks over an incredulous world, with no thought or care where they fell.

— Joan Bennett

How do people make it through

life without a sister?

—Sara Corpening

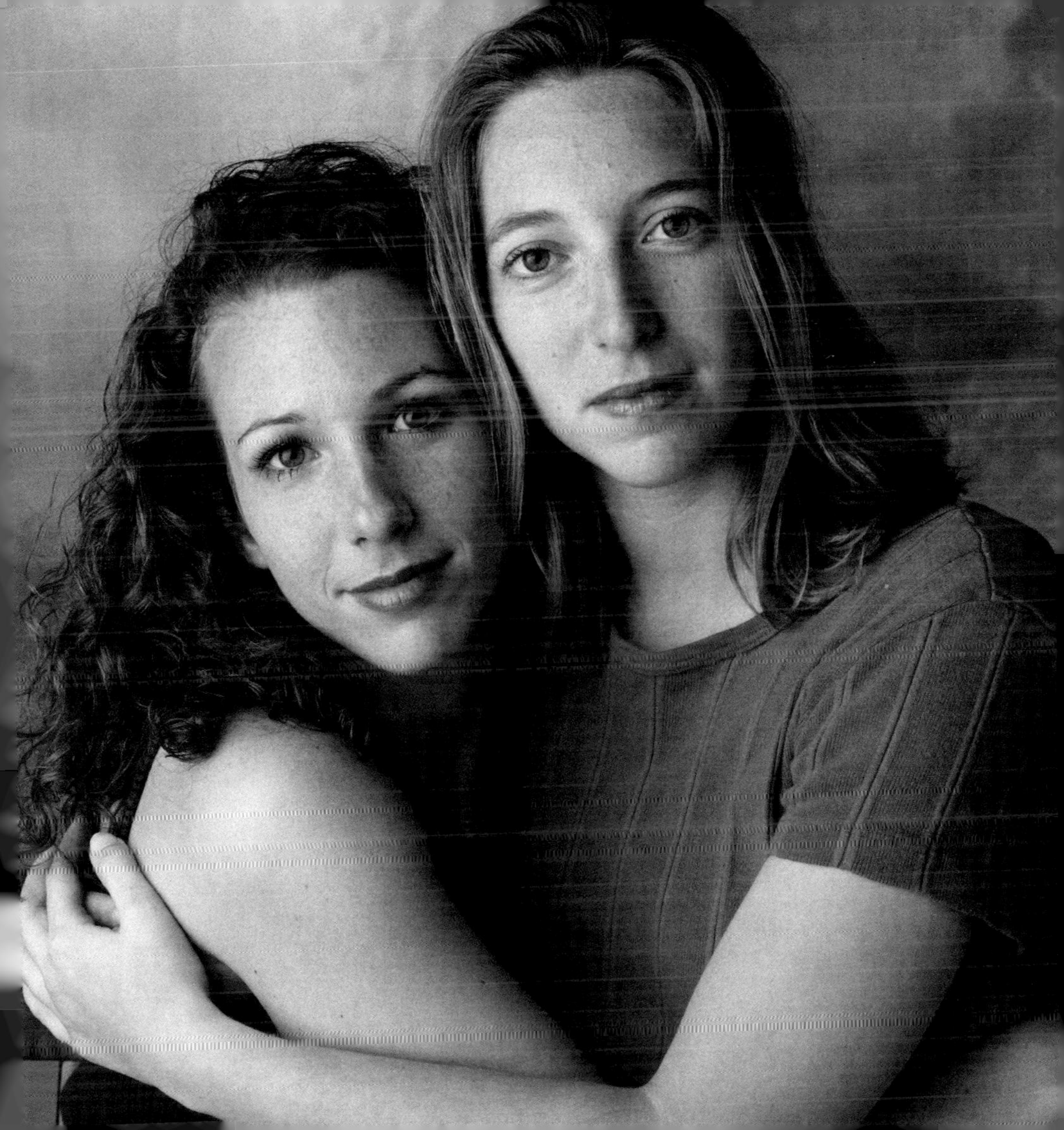

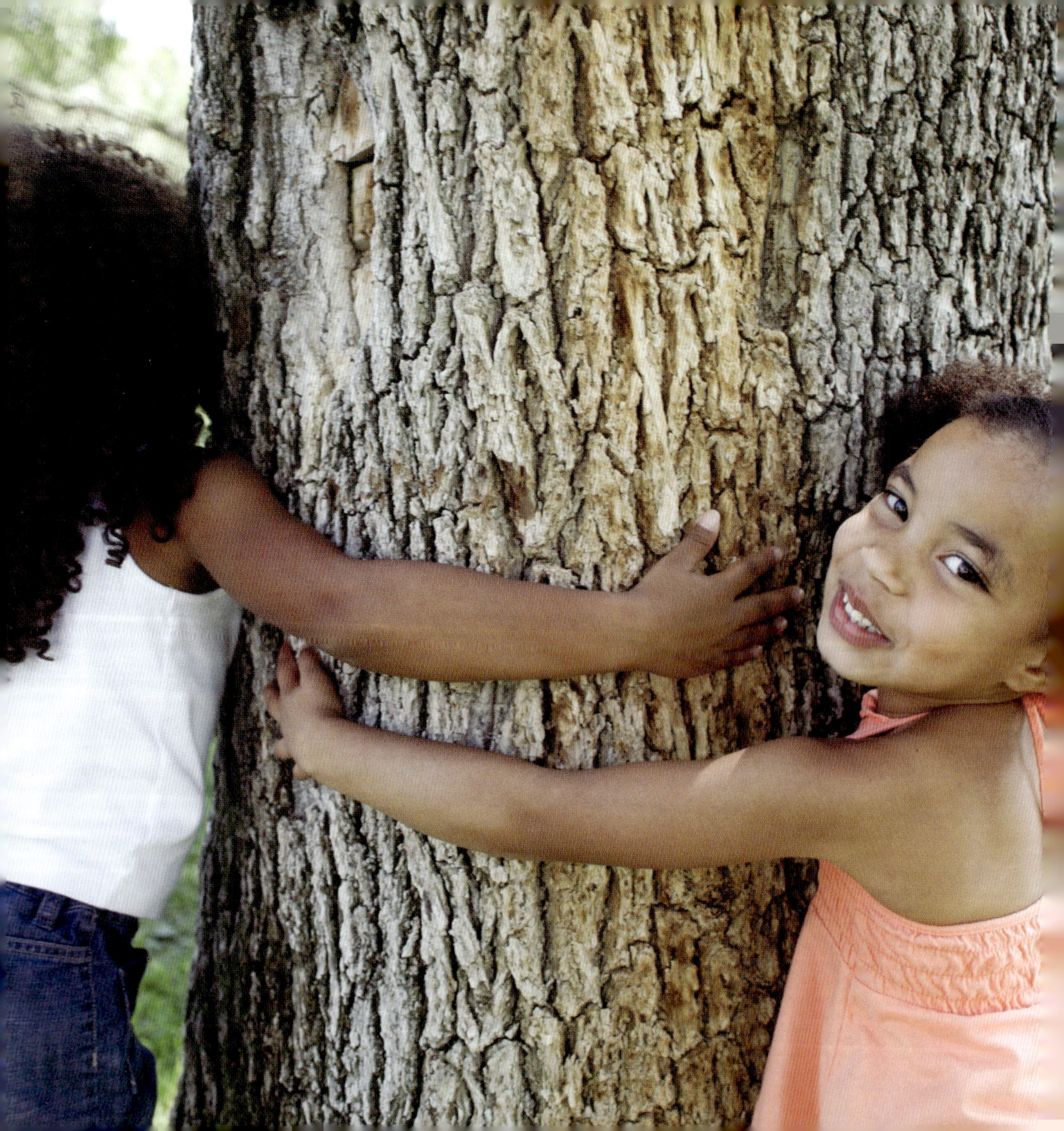

A SISTER CAN BE SEEN AS SOMEONE WHO IS BOTH OURSELVES AND VERY MUCH NOT OURSELVES—A SPECIAL KIND OF DOUBLE.

—Toni Morrison

IF SISTERS WERE FREE TO EXPRESS HOW THEY REALLY FEEL, PARENTS WOULD HEAR THIS: 'GIVE ME ALL THE ATTENTION AND ALL THE TOYS AND SEND REBECCA TO LIVE WITH GRANDMA.'

— Linda Sunshine

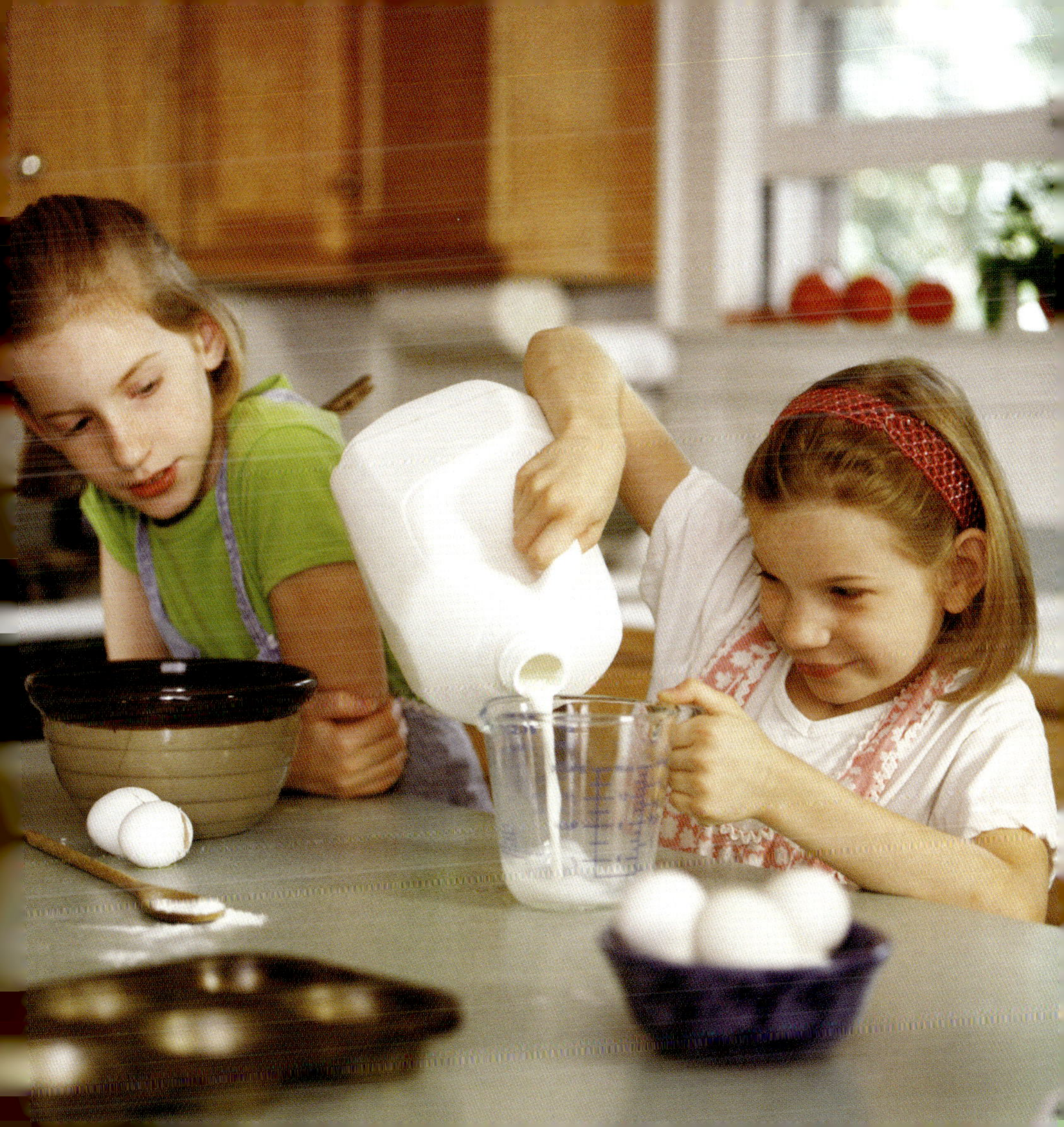

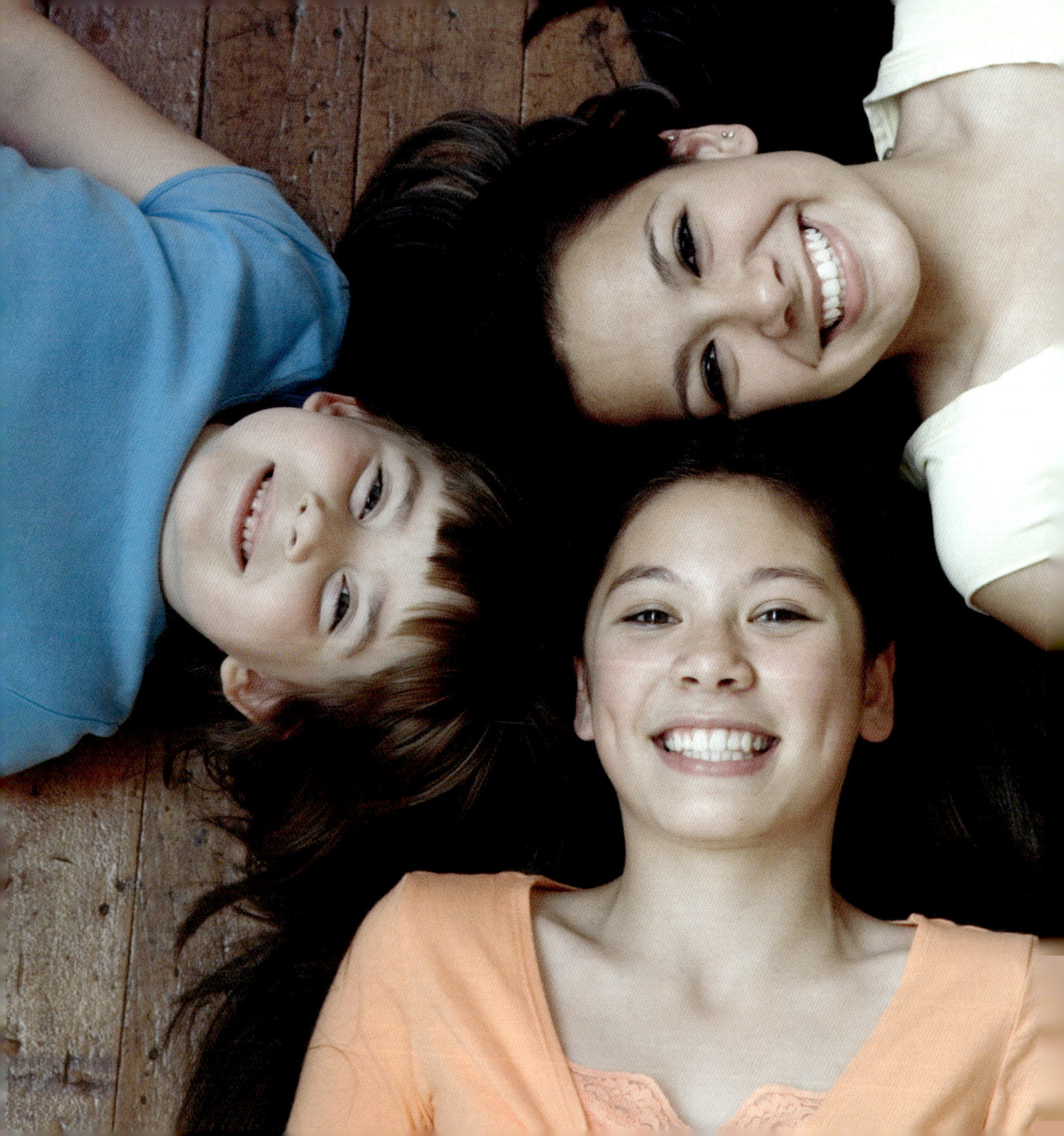

I sought my soul,

But I could not see.

I sought my God,

But God eluded me.

I sought my sisters,

And found all three.

Author Unknown

BOTH WITHIN THE FAMILY AND WITHOUT,

OUR SISTERS HOLD UP OUR MIRRORS:

OUR IMAGES OF WHO WE ARE AND OF

WHO WE CAN DARE TO BECOME.

—Elizabeth Fishel

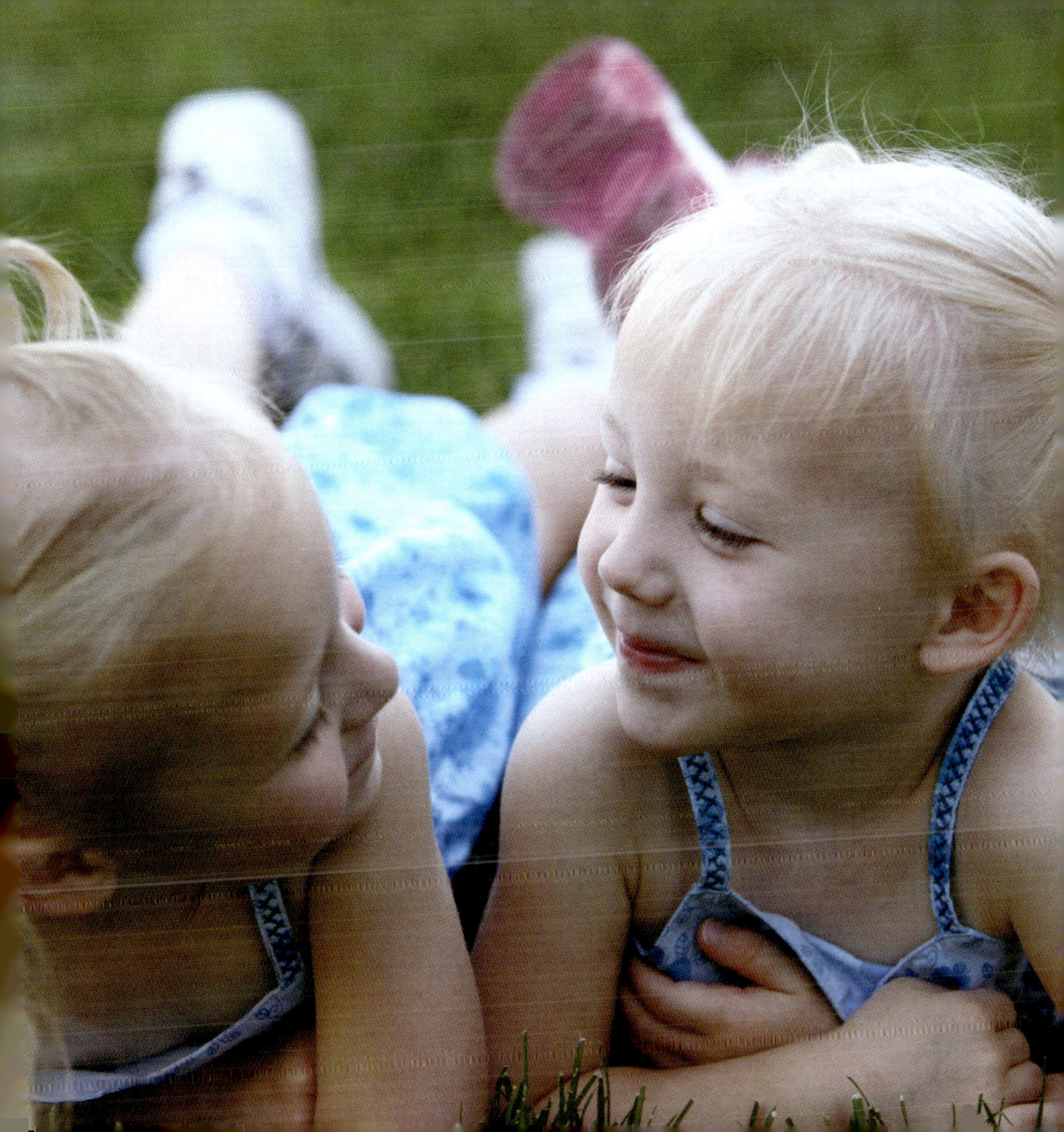

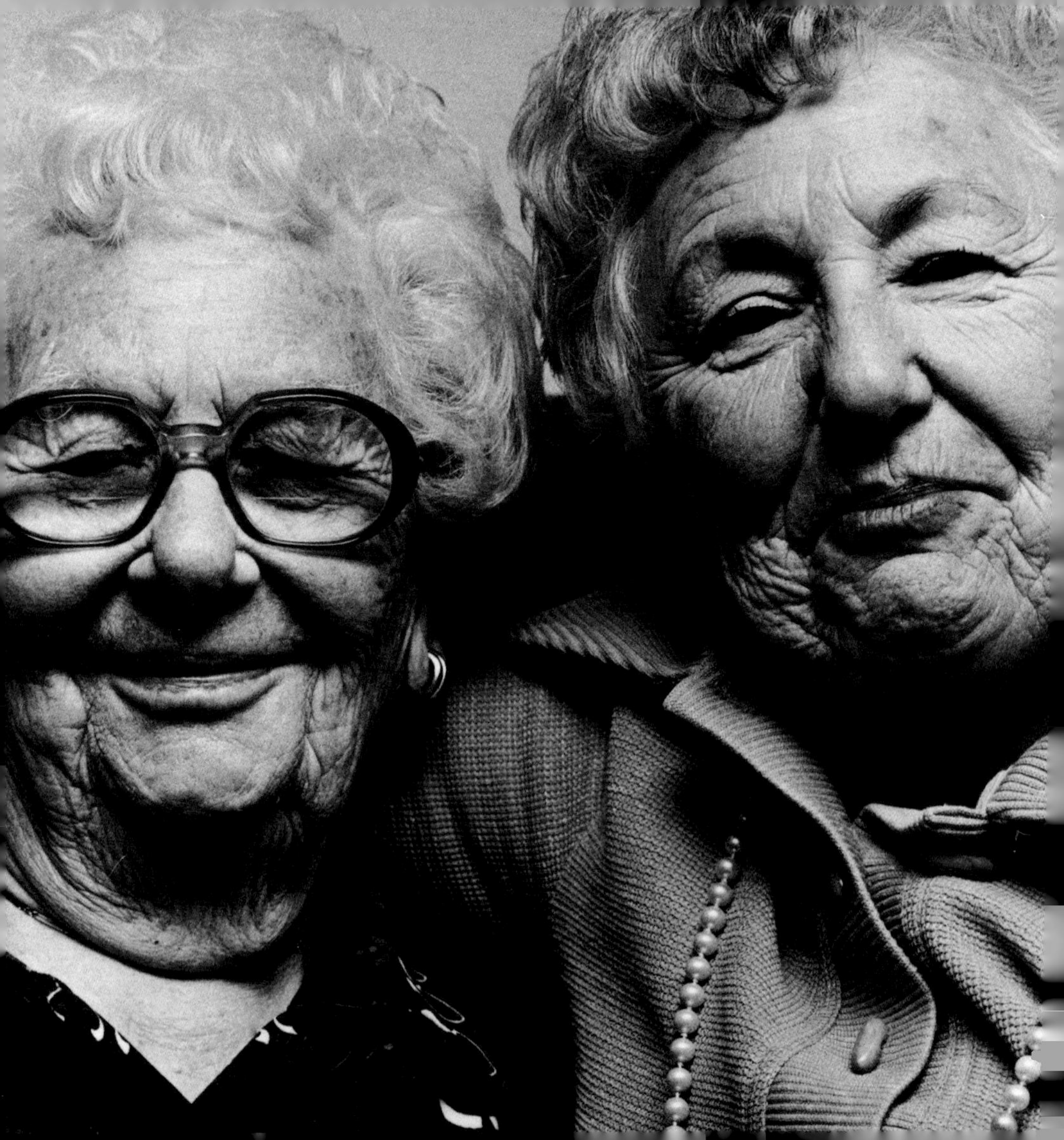

Our sisters push buttons that cast us in roles we felt sure we had let go of long ago—the baby, the peacekeeper, the caretaker, the avoider.... It doesn't seem to matter how much time has elapsed, or how far we've traveled.

—Jane Mersky Leder

Bless you, my darling, and remember you are always in the heart—tucked so close there is no chance of escape—of your sister.

— Katherine Mansfield

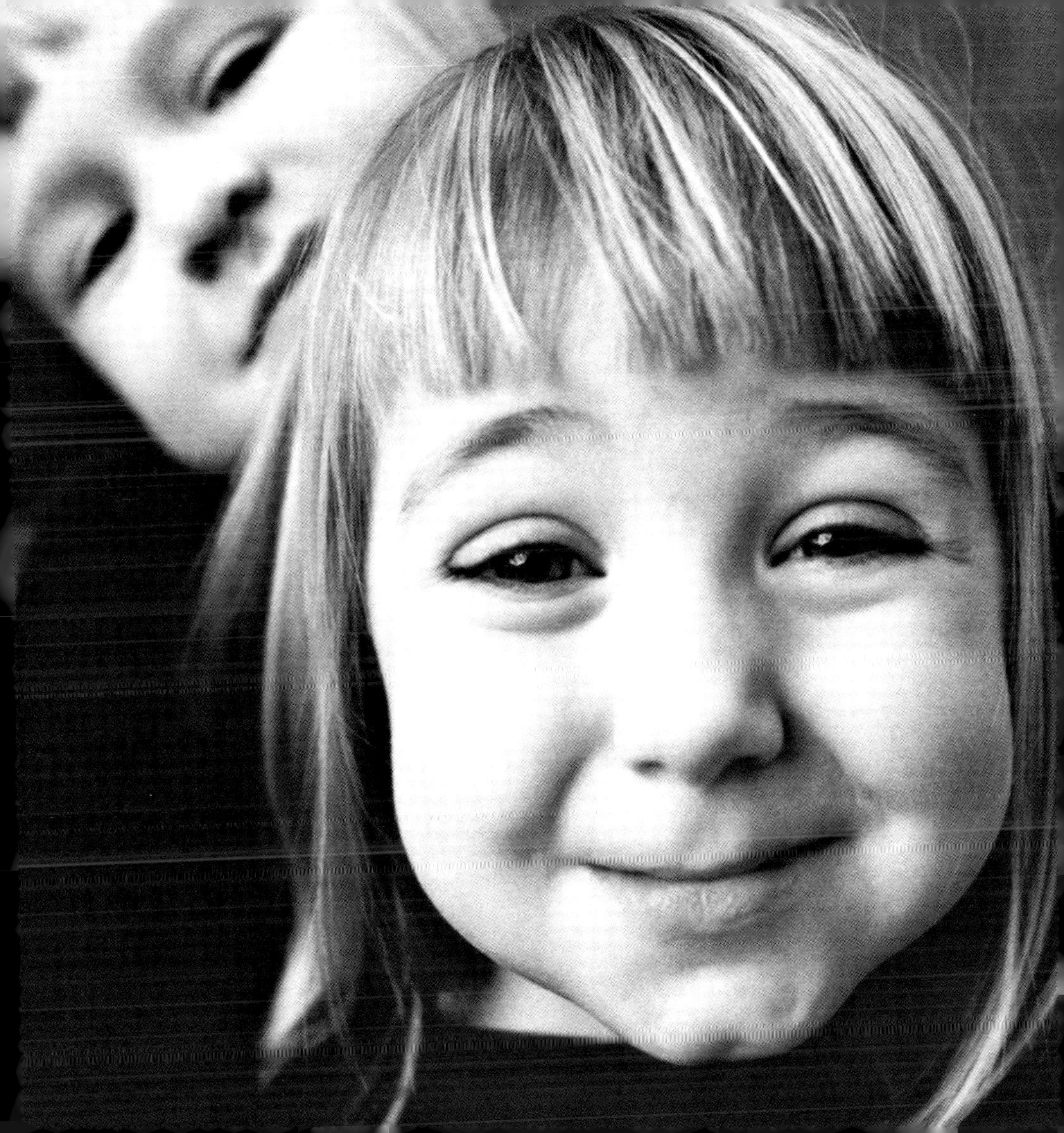

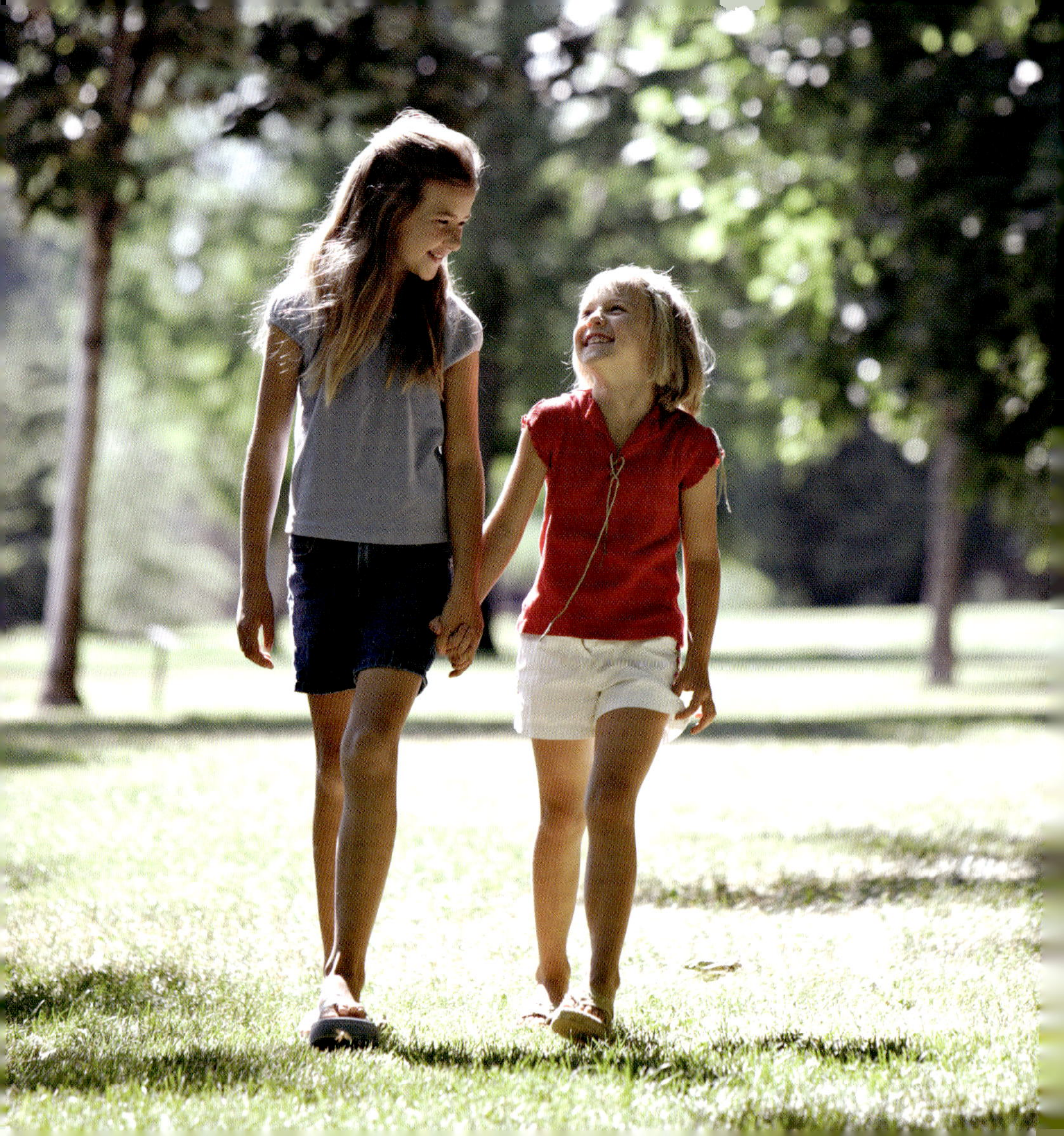

SHE TAKES MY HAND AND LEADS ME ALONG PATHS

I WOULD NOT HAVE DARED EXPLORE ALONE.

— Maya V. Patel

You can kid the world,

but not your sister.

— Charlotte Gray

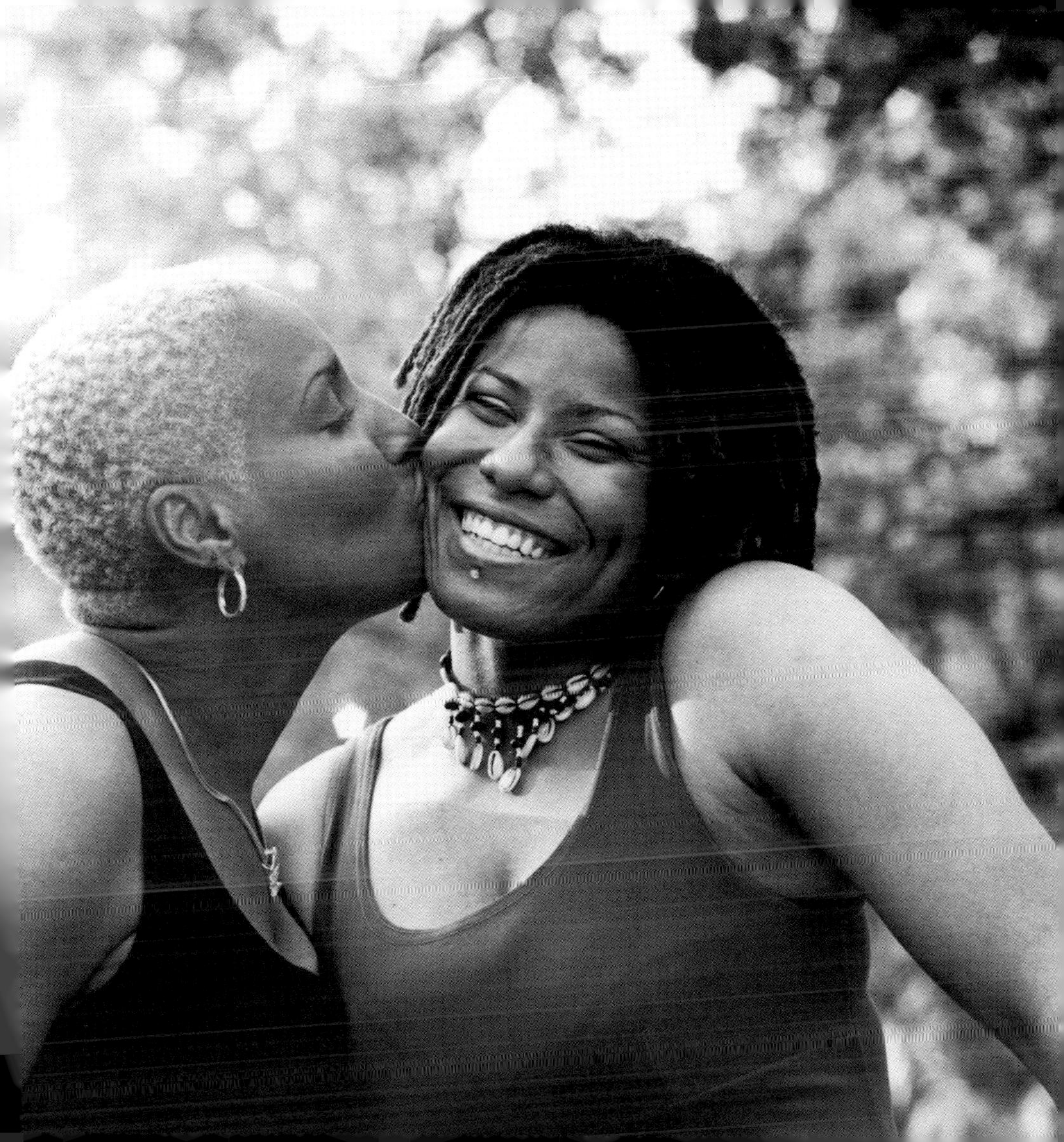

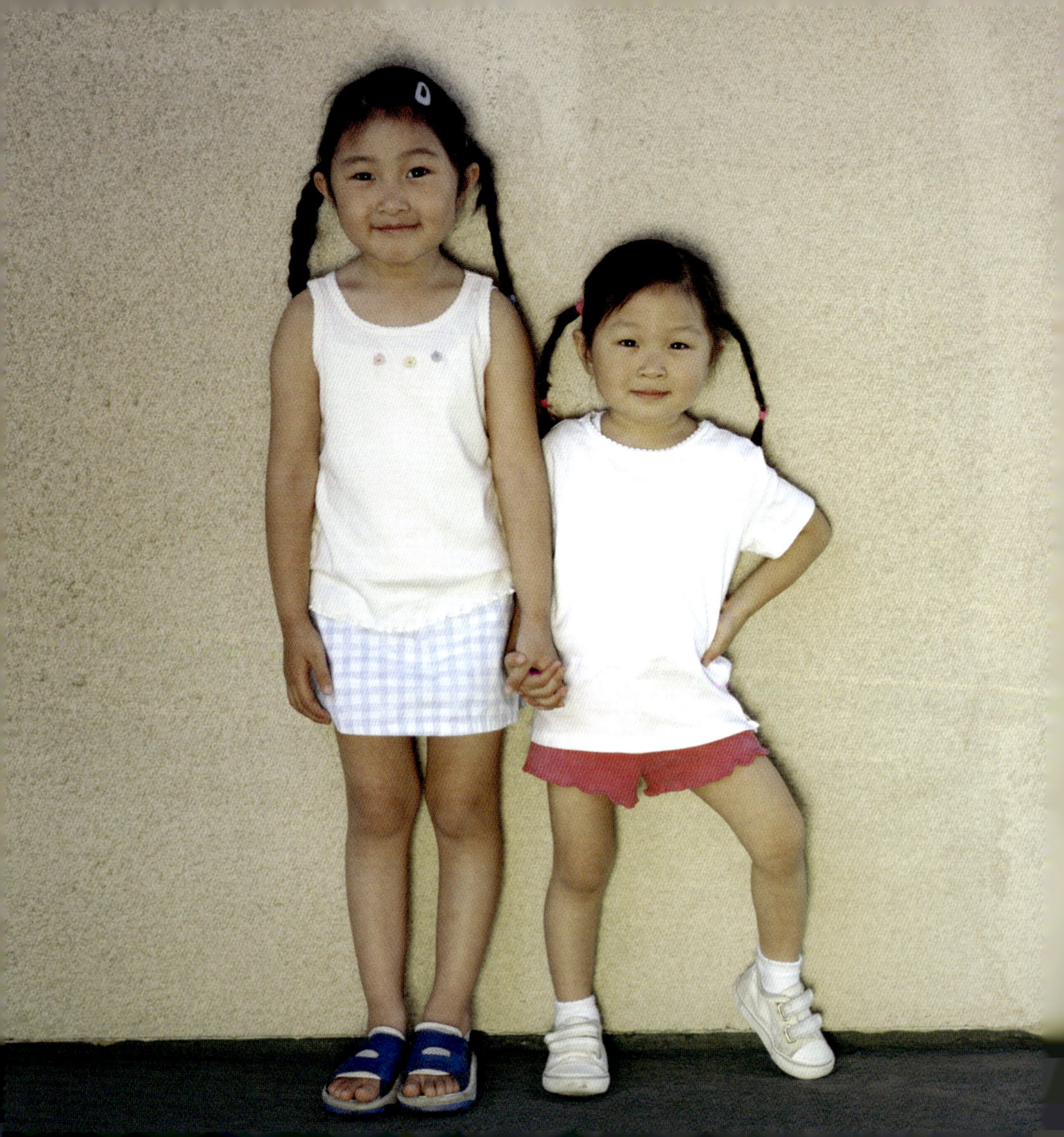

Sisters touch your heart in ways no other could.

Sisters share... their hopes, their fears, their love,

everything they have. Real friendship

springs from their special bonds.

—Carrie Bagwell

THE MILDEST, CALMEST SISTER HAS BEEN KNOWN TO TURN INTO A TIGER IF HER SIBLING IS IN TROUBLE.

— Clara Ortega

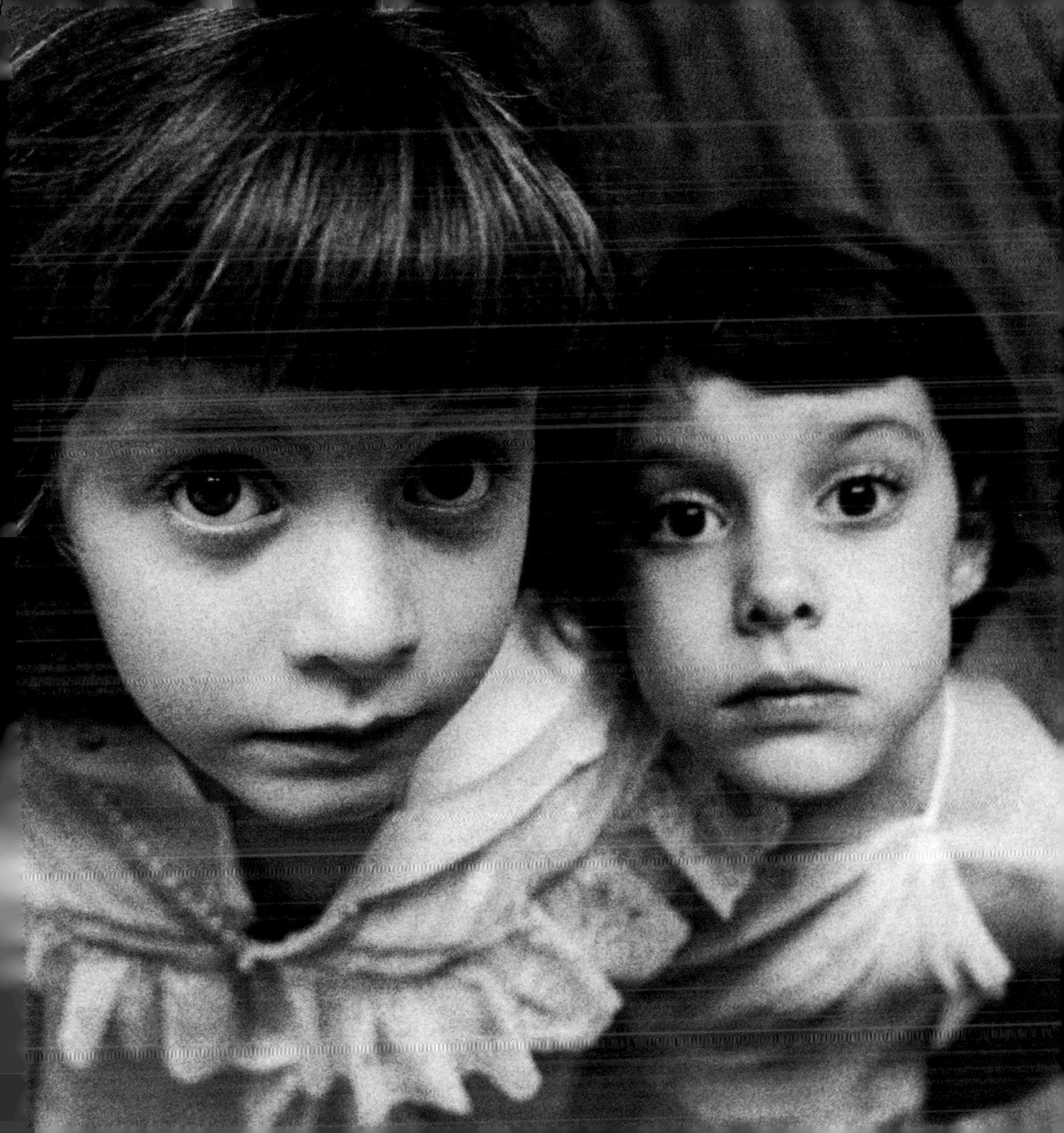

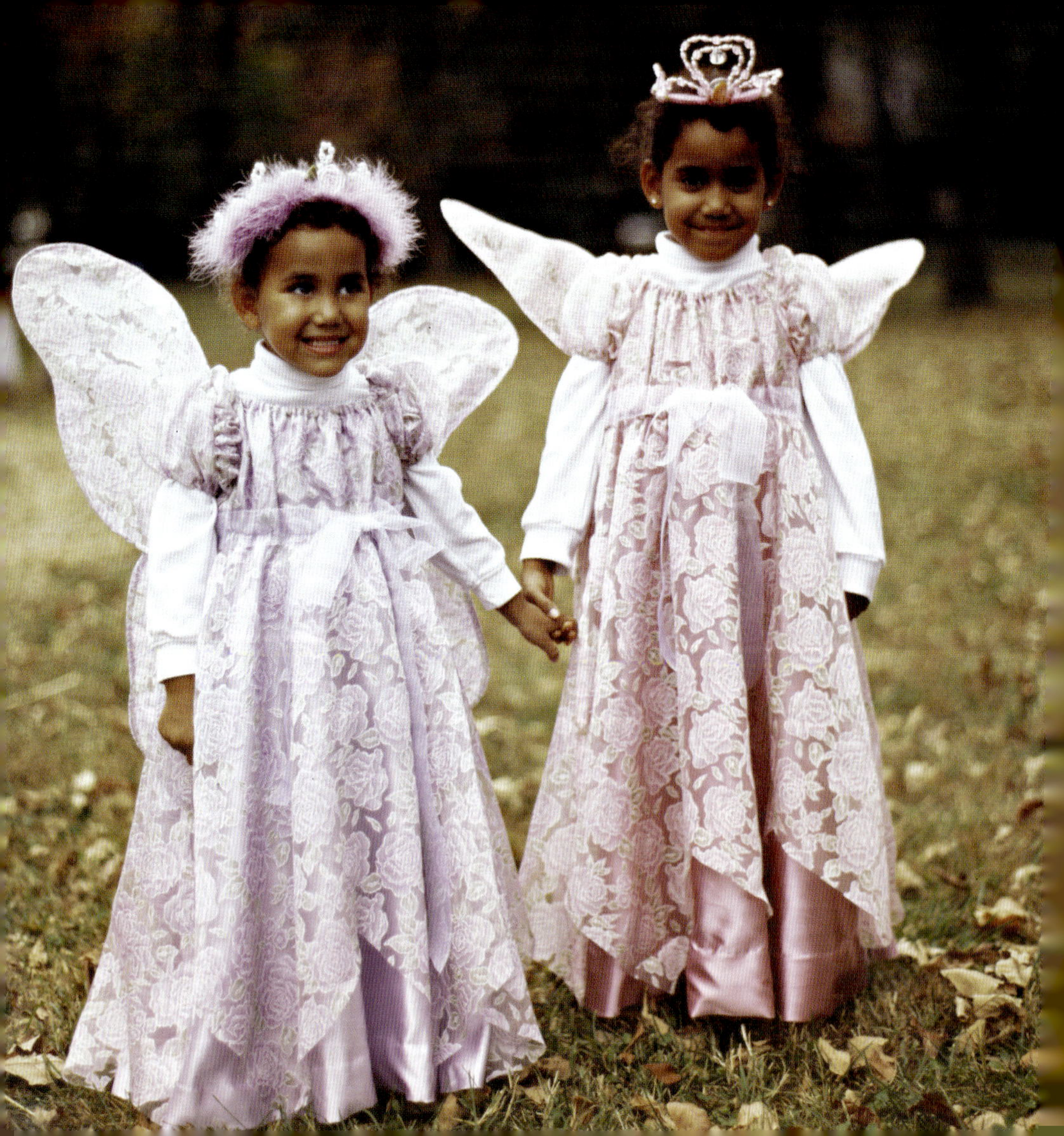

THE BEST THING ABOUT HAVING A SISTER

WAS THAT I ALWAYS HAD A FRIEND.

—Cali Rae Turner

We ACQUIRE FRIENDS AND WE MAKE ENEMIES,

BUT OUR SISTERS COME WITH THE TERRITORY.

— Evelyn Loeb

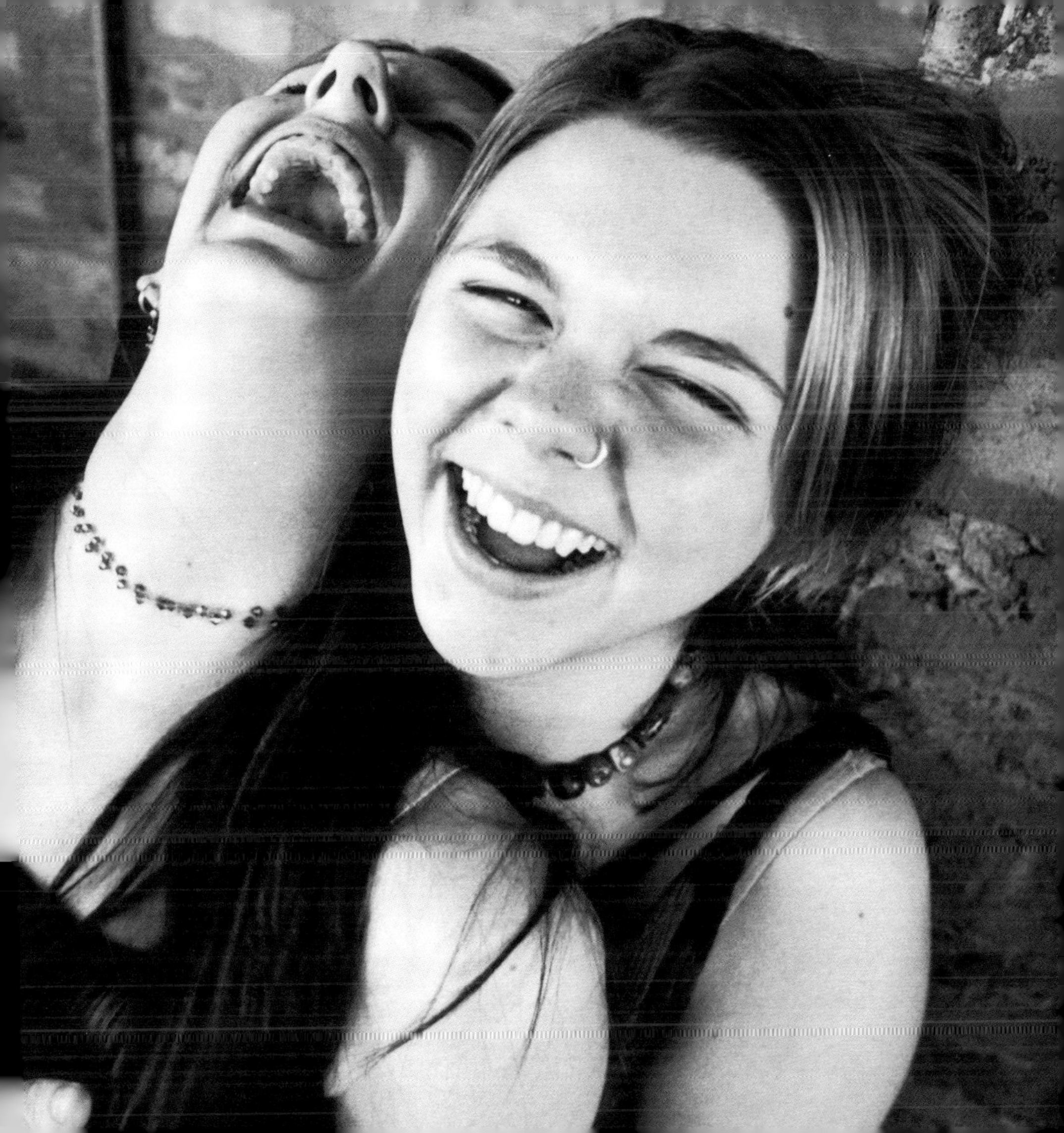

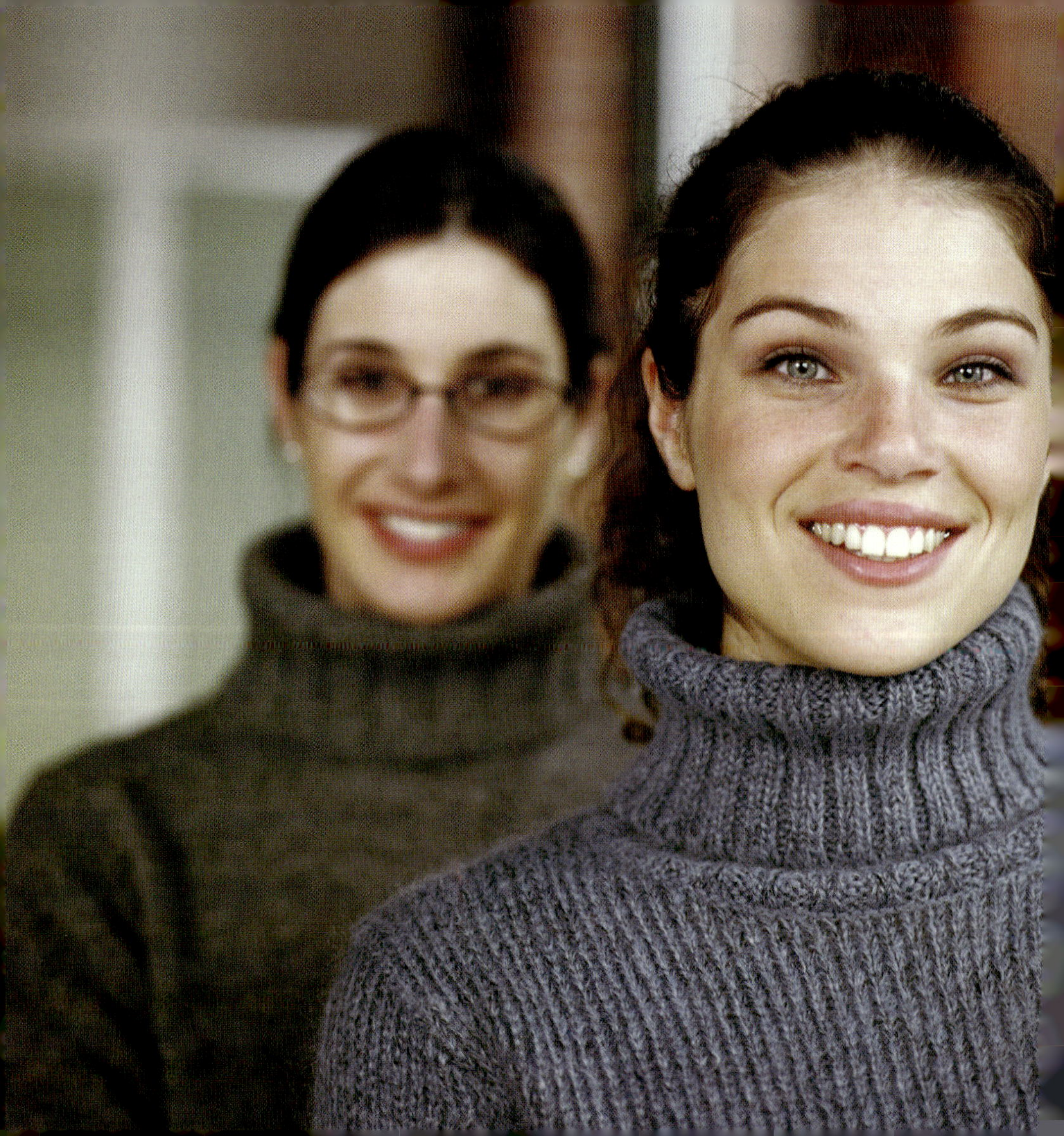

IF YOU DON'T UNDERSTAND HOW A WOMAN COULD BOTH LOVE HER SISTER DEARLY AND WANT TO WRING HER NECK AT THE SAME TIME, THEN YOU WERE PROBABLY AN ONLY CHILD.

—Linda Sunshine

An older sister is a friend and defender—

a listener, conspirator, a counselor and

a sharer of delights and sorrows.

—Author Unknown

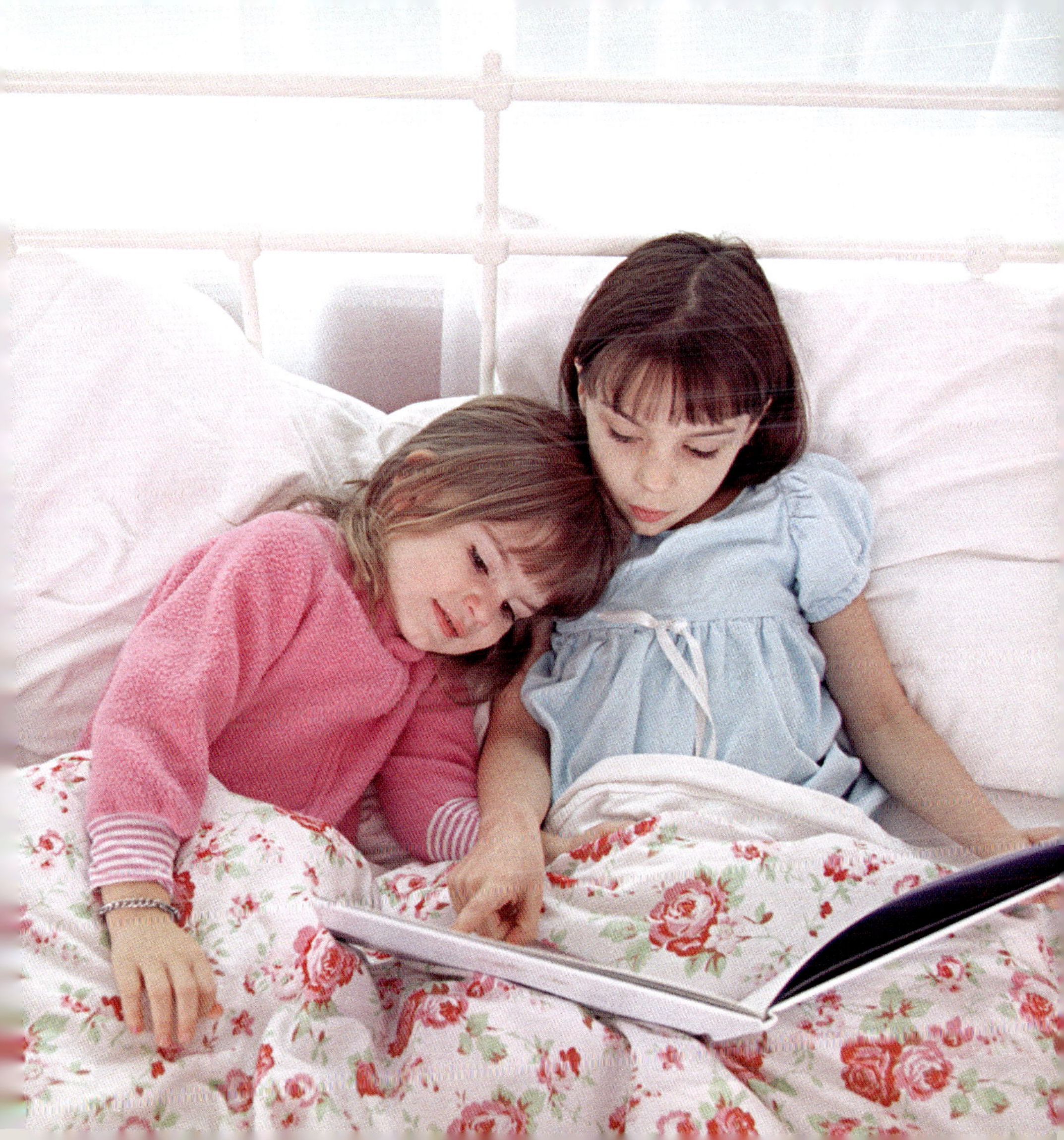

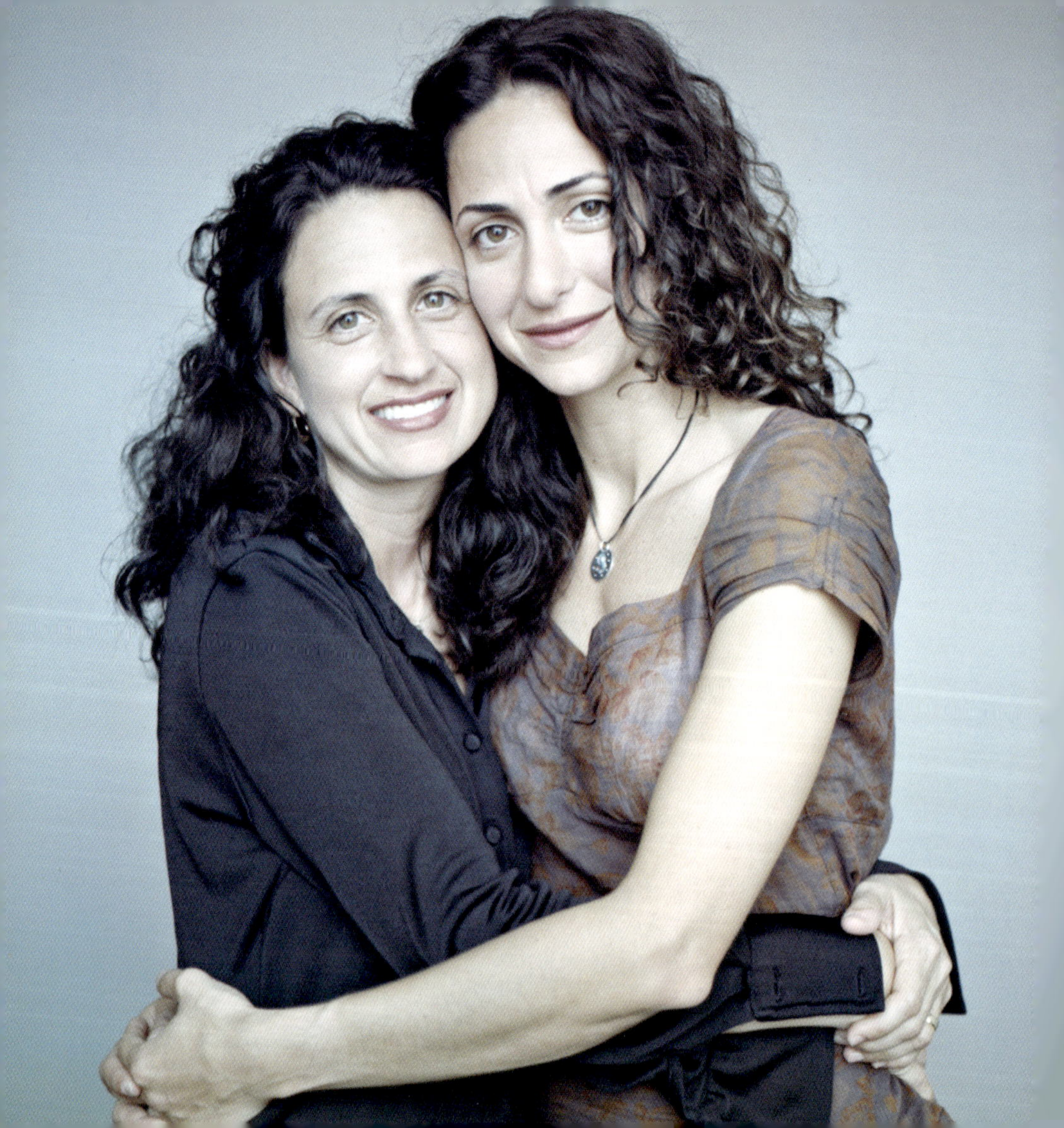

Is solace anywhere more comforting

than in the arms of a sister?

— Alice Walker

In thee my soul

Shall own combined

The sister and the friend.

— Catherine Killigrew

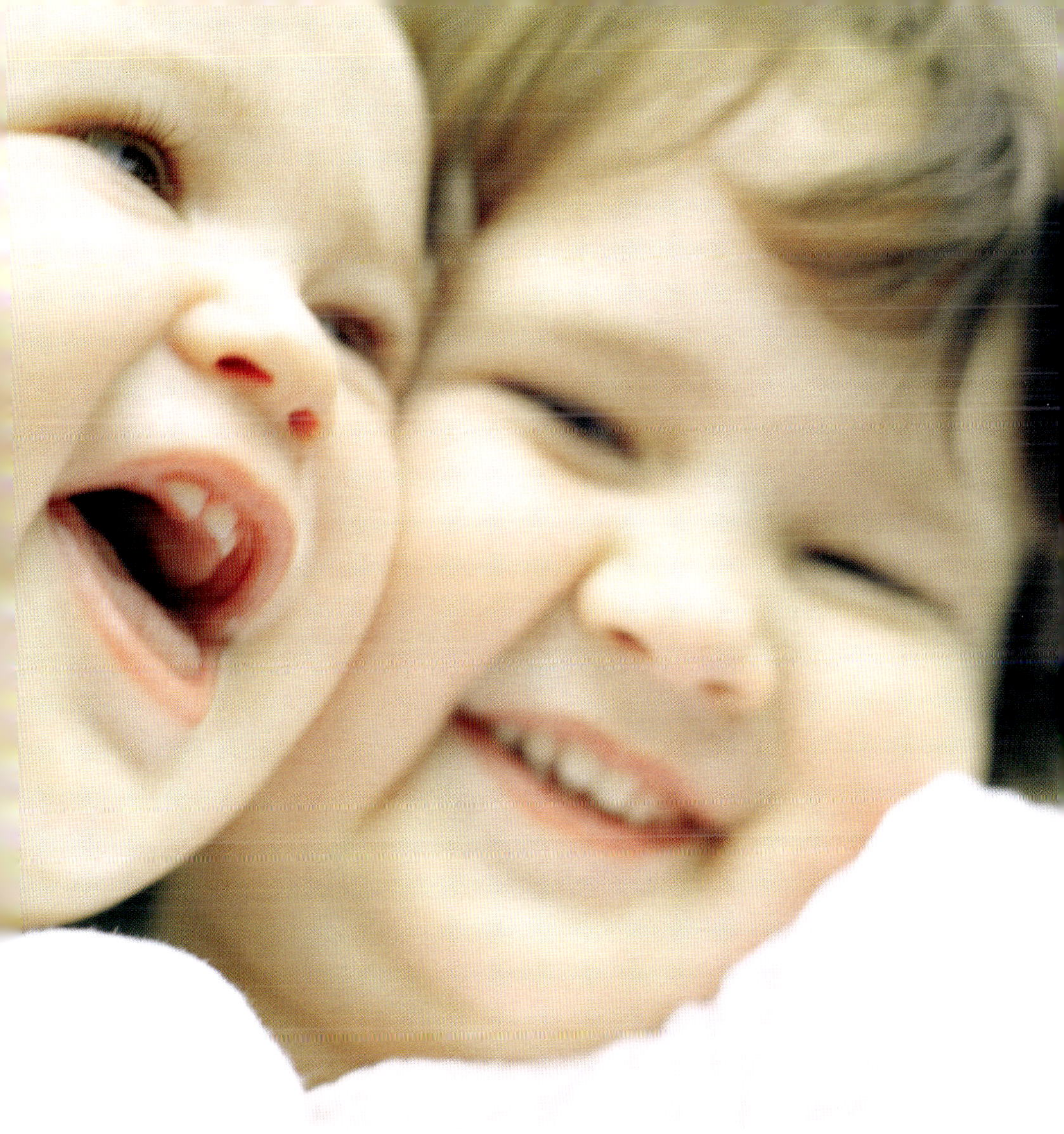

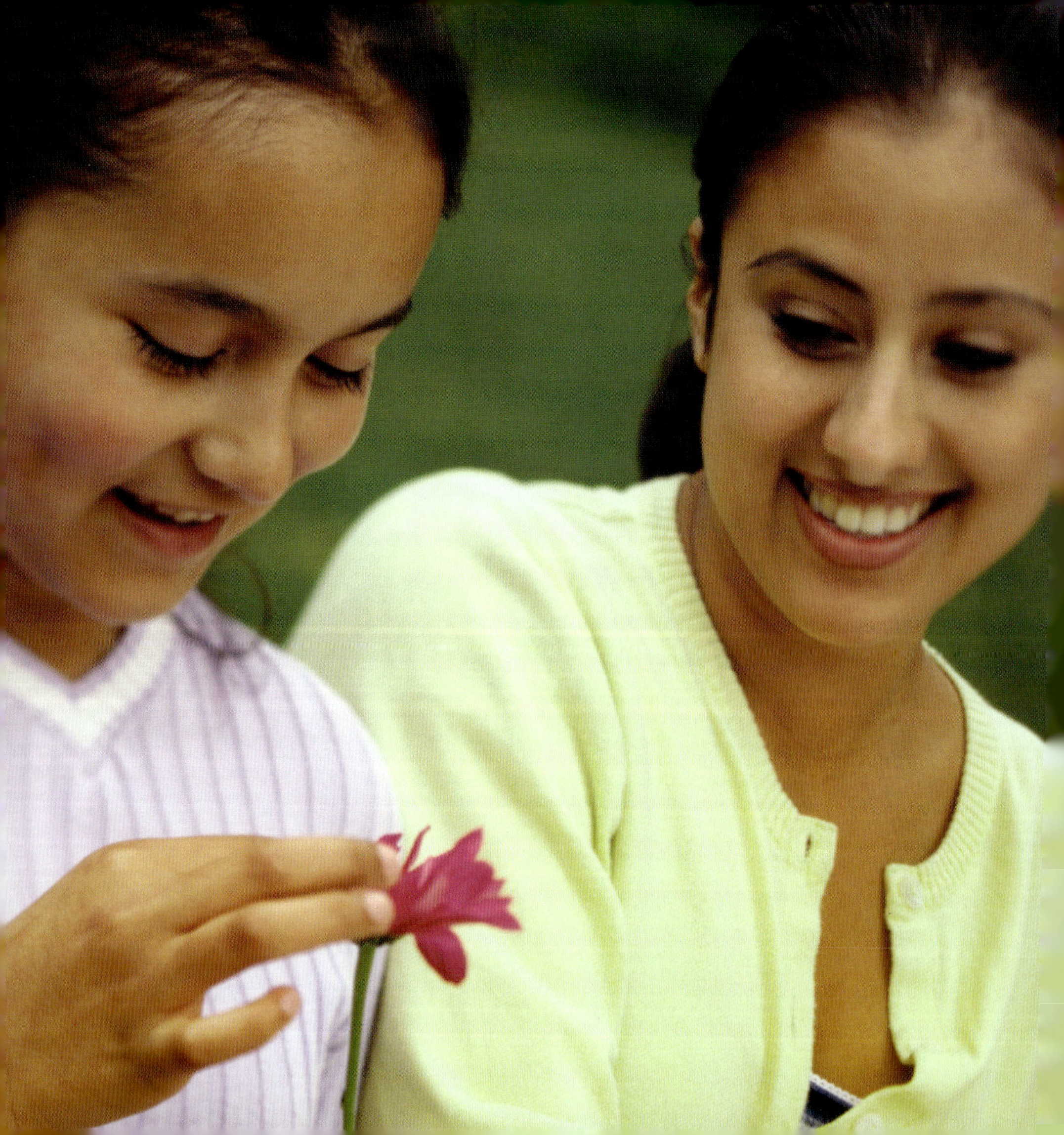

For there is no friend like a sister

In calm or stormy weather;

To cheer one on the tedious way,

To fetch one if one goes astray,

To lift one if one totters down,

To strengthen whilst one stands.

— Christina Rossetti

There can be no situation in life in which the conversation of my dear sister will not administer some comfort to me.

— Mary Montagu

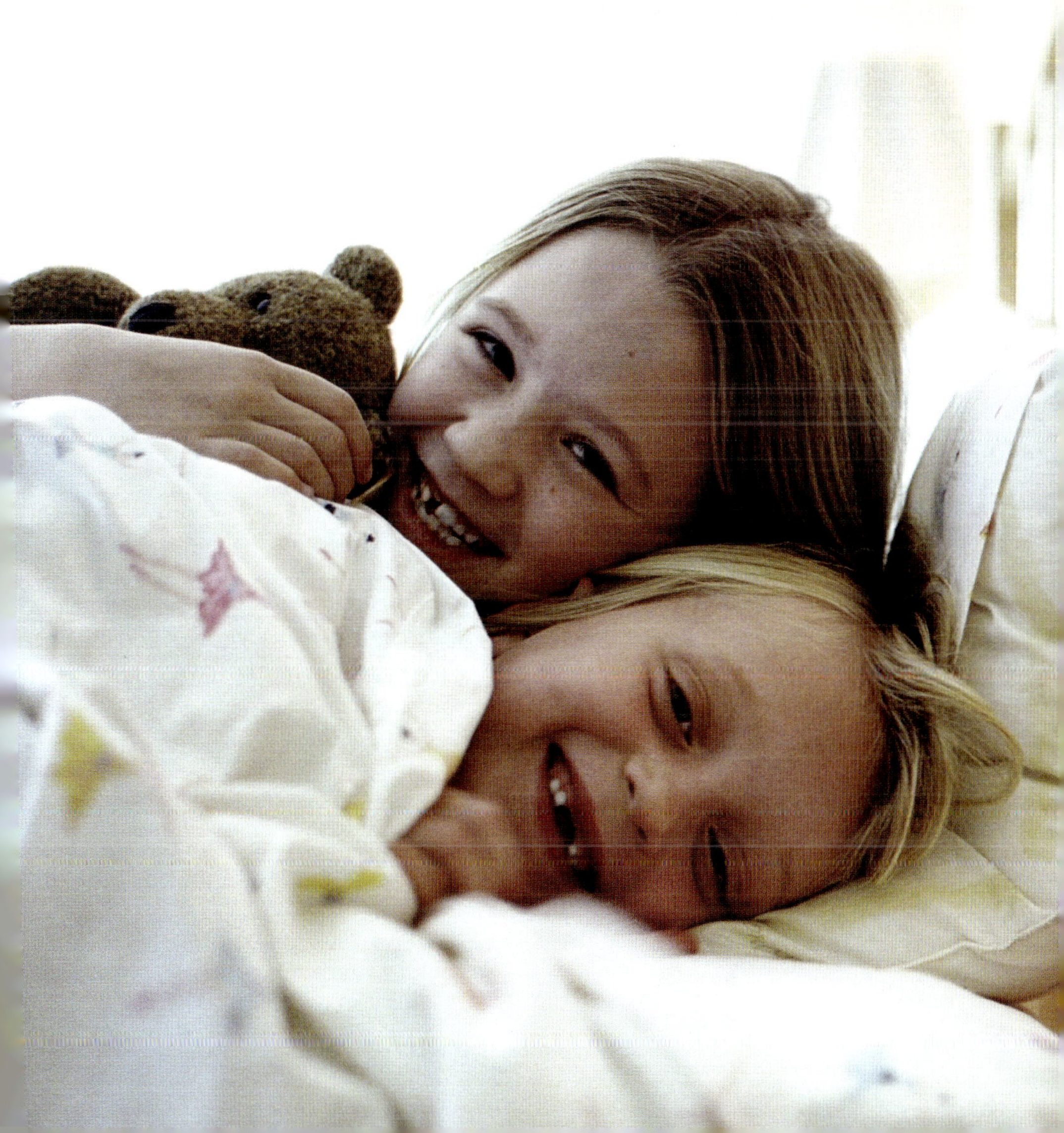

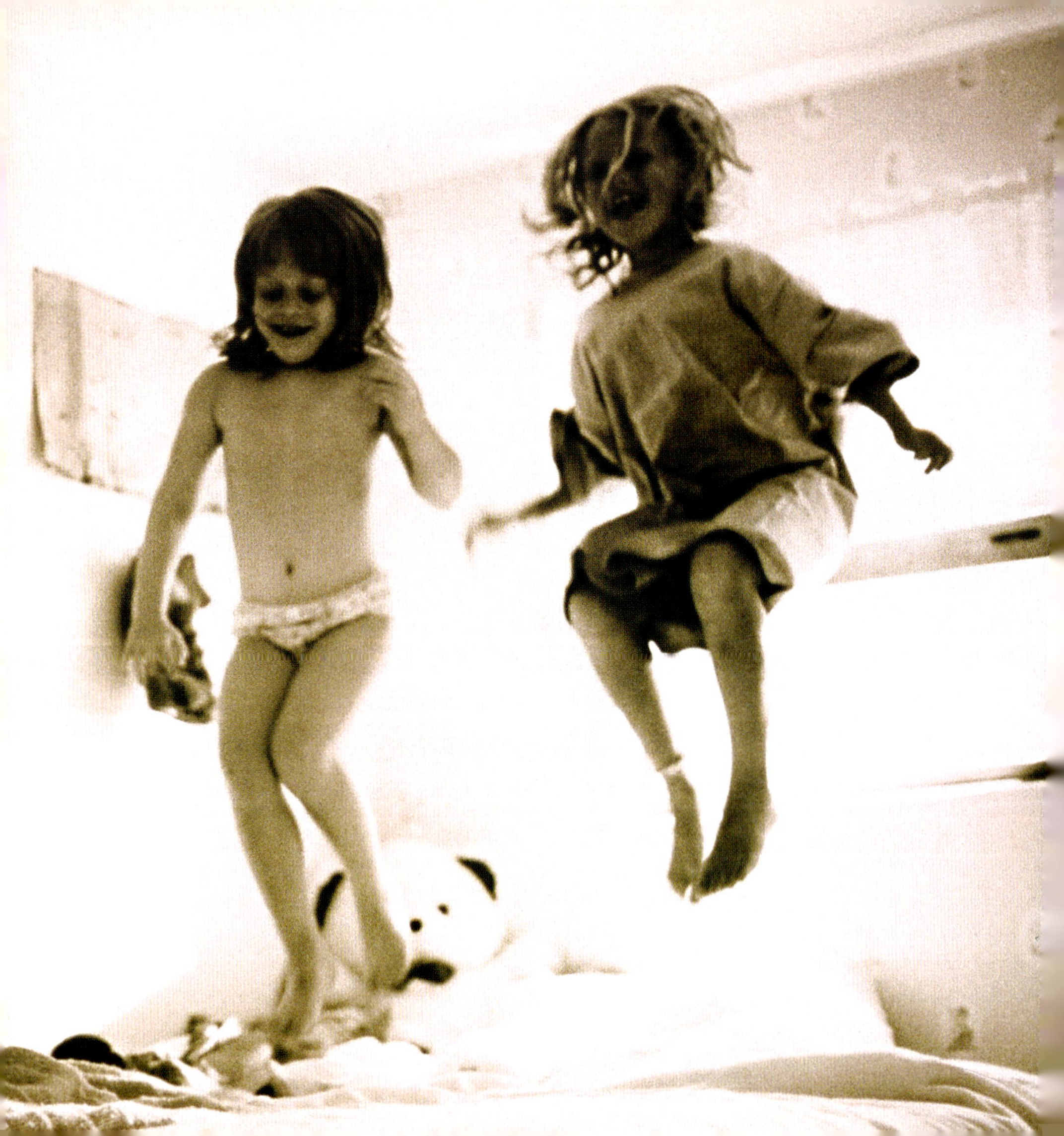

There's a special kind of freedom sisters enjoy.

Freedom to share innermost thoughts, to ask a favor,

to show their true feelings. The freedom to

simply be themselves.

—Author Unknown

Your sister is your other self.

She is your alter ego, your reflection,

your foil, your shadow.

— Barbara Mathias

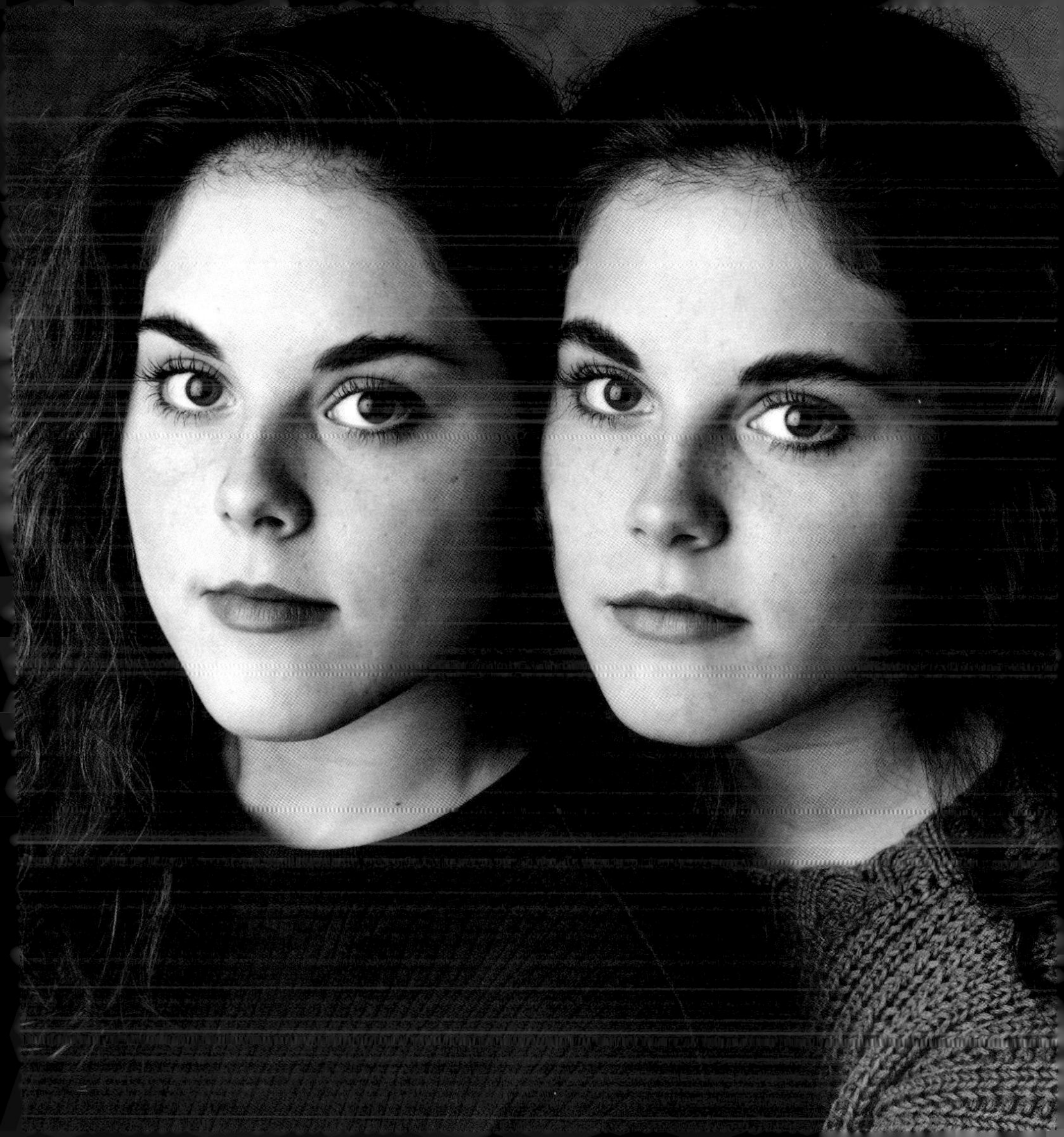

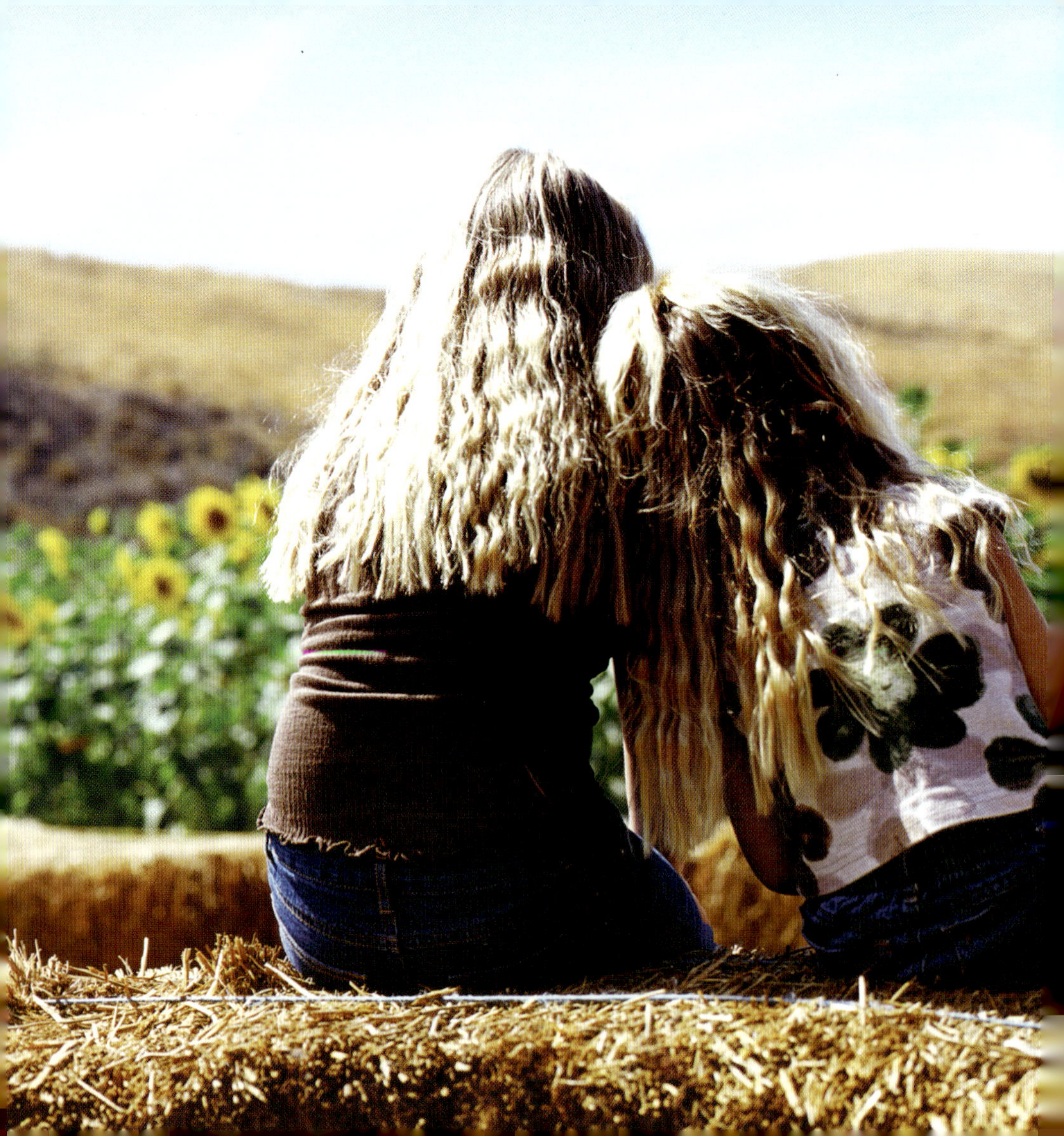

Helping one another is part of

the religion of sisterhood.

— Louisa May Alcott

Sisters don't need words. They have perfected a language of snarls and smiles and frowns and winks—expressions of shocked surprise and incredulity and disbelief. Sniffs and snorts and gasps and sighs—that can undermine any tale you're telling.

—Author Unknown

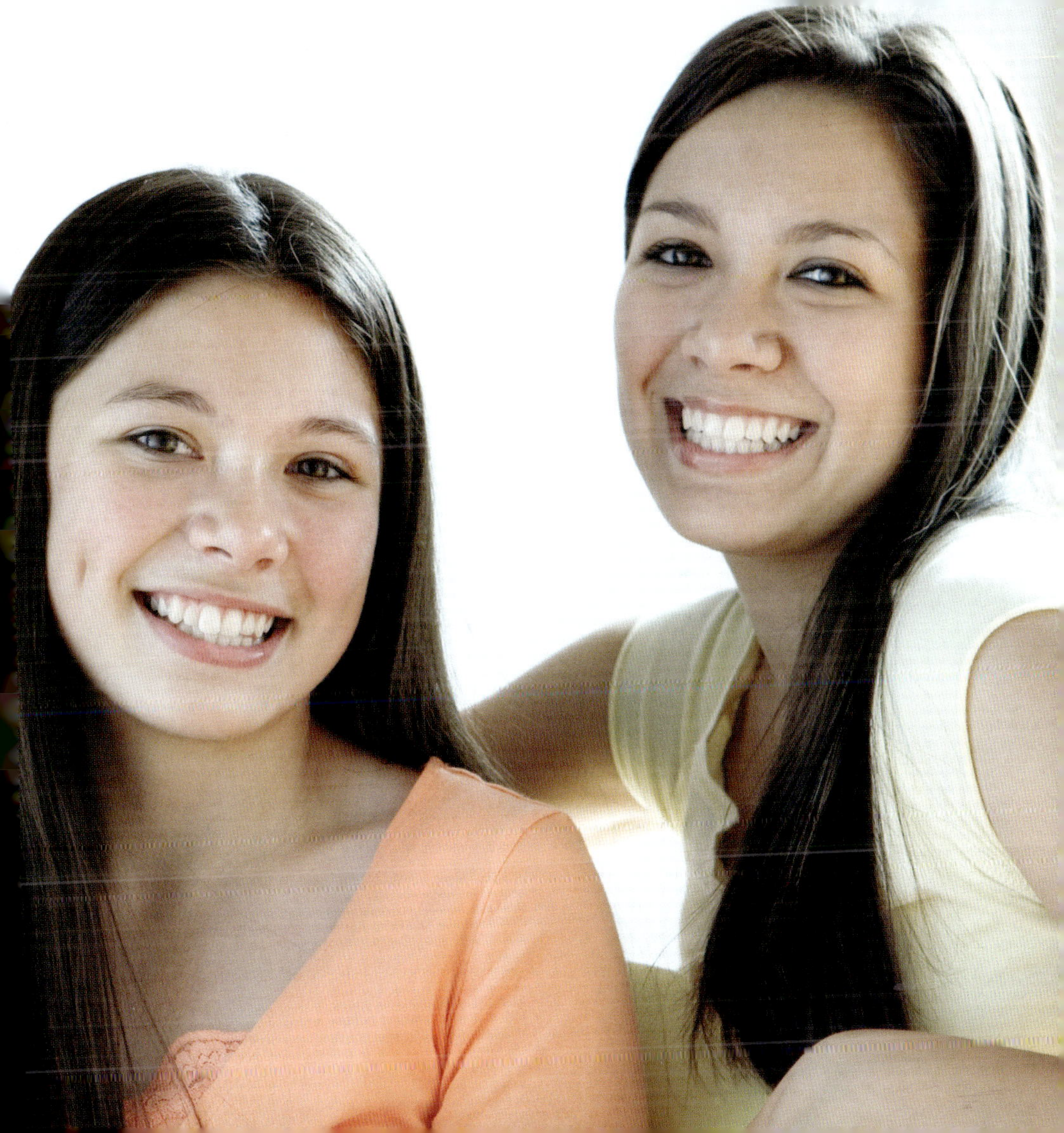

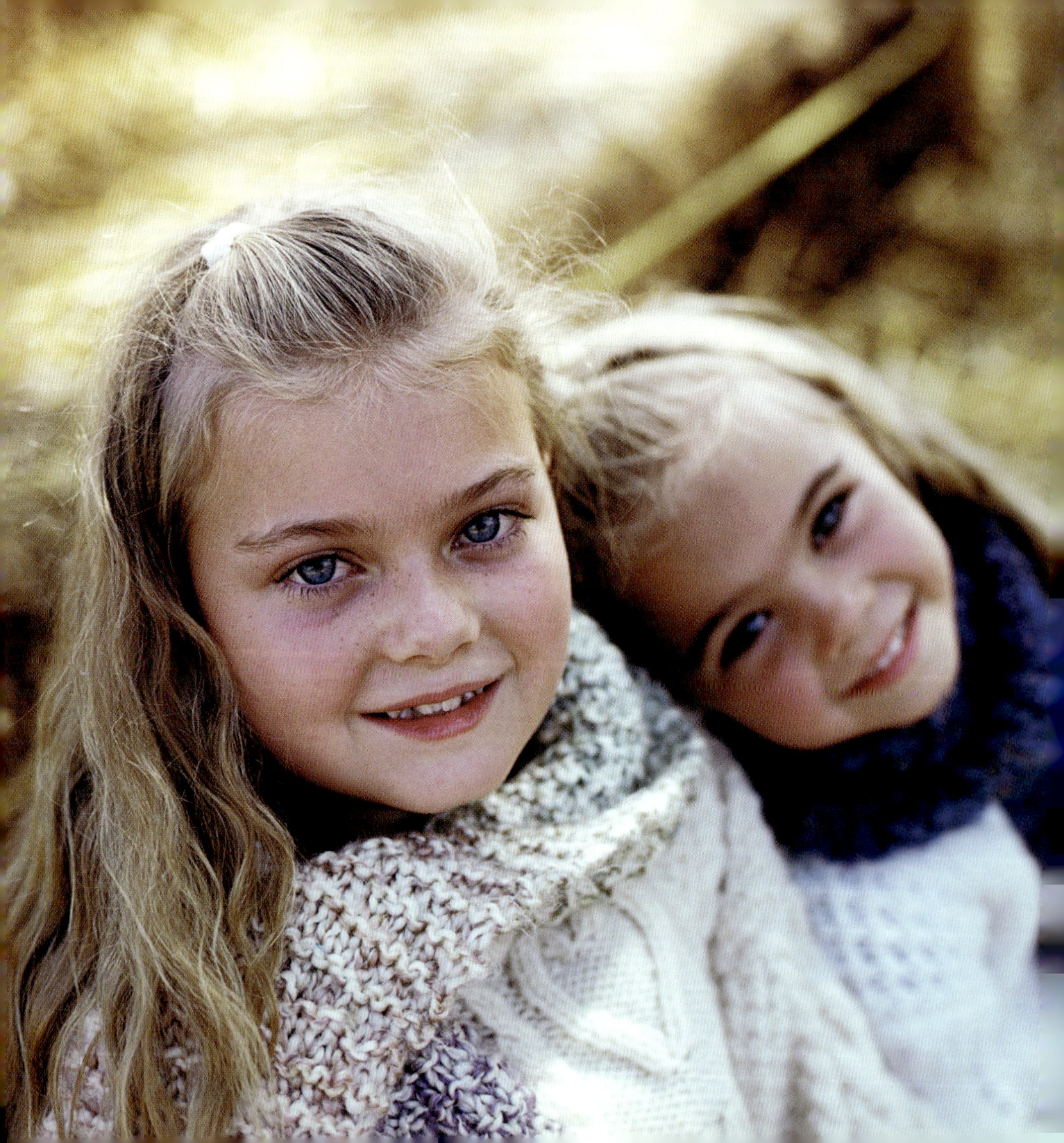

ONE OF THE BEST THINGS ABOUT BEING AN ADULT

IS THE REALIZATION THAT YOU CAN SHARE WITH

YOUR SISTER AND STILL HAVE PLENTY FOR YOURSELF.

Betsy Cohen

I KNOW SOME SISTERS WHO ONLY SEE EACH OTHER ON MOTHER'S DAY AND SOME WHO WILL NEVER SPEAK AGAIN. BUT MOST ARE LIKE MY SISTER AND ME...LINKED BY VOLATILE LOVE, BEST FRIENDS WHO MAKE OTHER BEST FRIENDS EVER SO SLIGHTLY LESS BEST.

— Patricia Volk

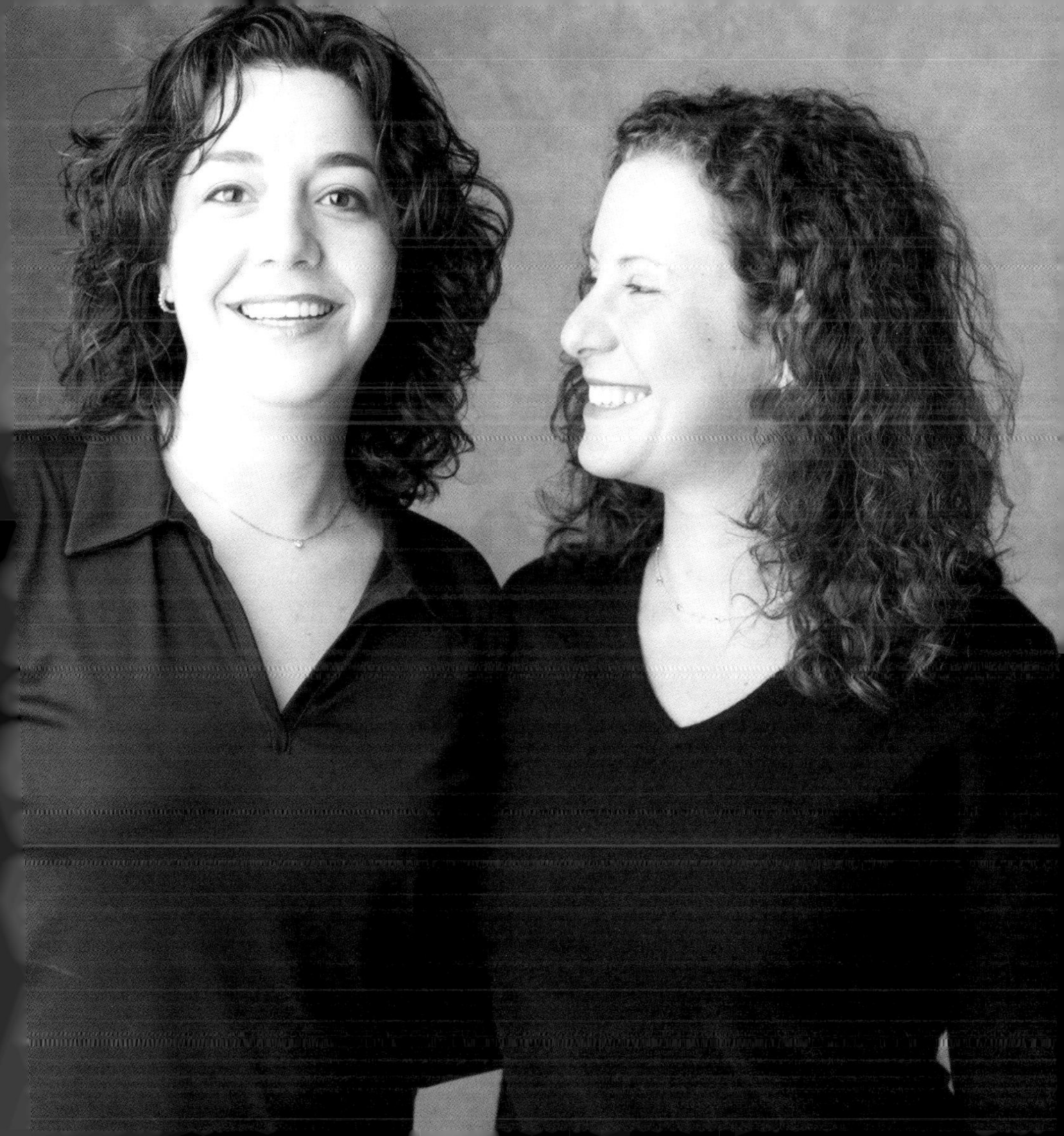

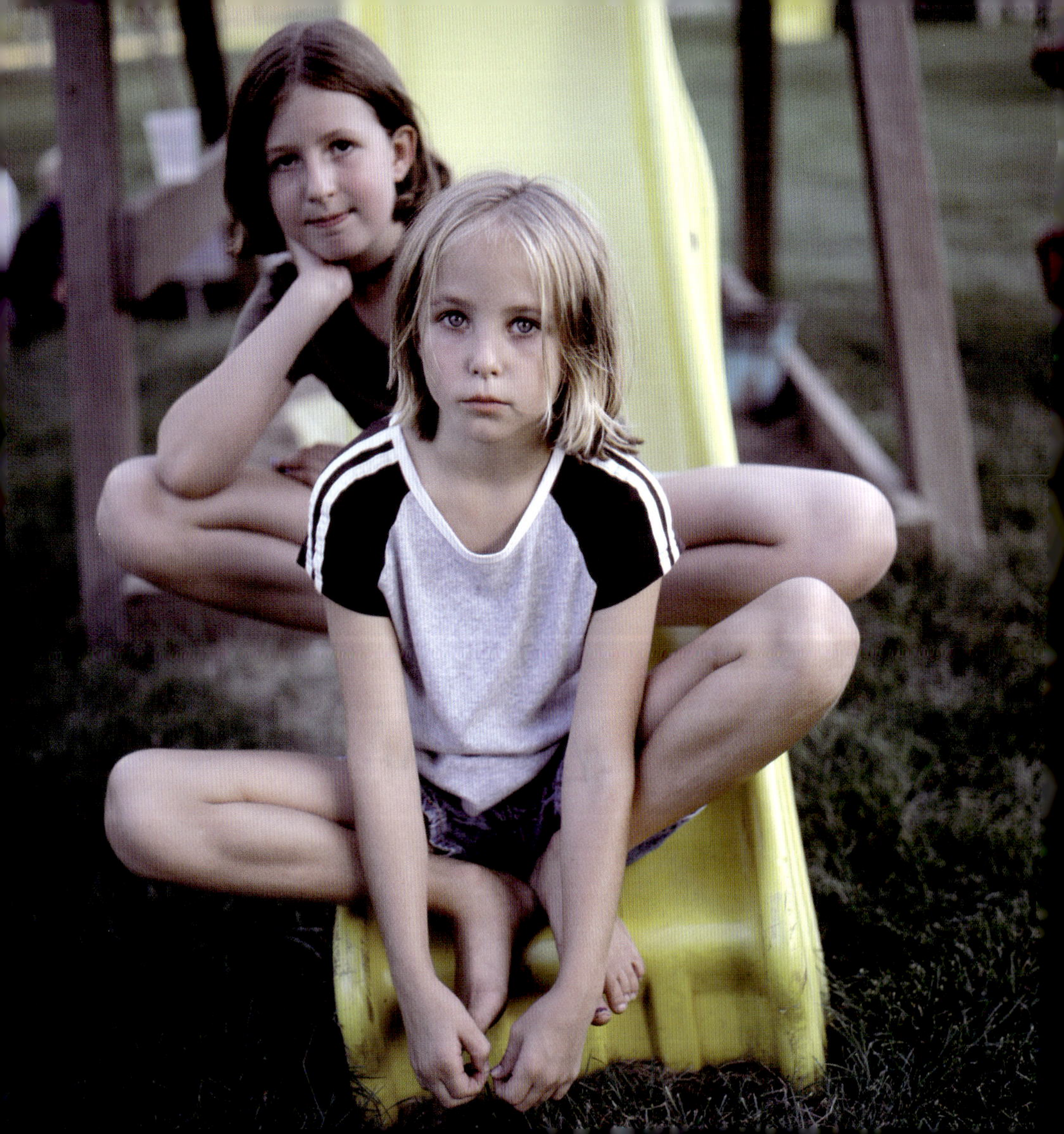

WE KNOW ONE ANOTHER'S FAULTS, VIRTUES,

CATASTROPHES, MORTIFICATIONS, TRIUMPHS,

RIVALRIES, DESIRES, AND HOW LONG WE CAN

EACH HANG BY OUR HANDS TO A BAR.

—Rose Macaulay

We may look old and wise to the outside world.

But to each other, we are still in junior school.

— Charlotte Gray

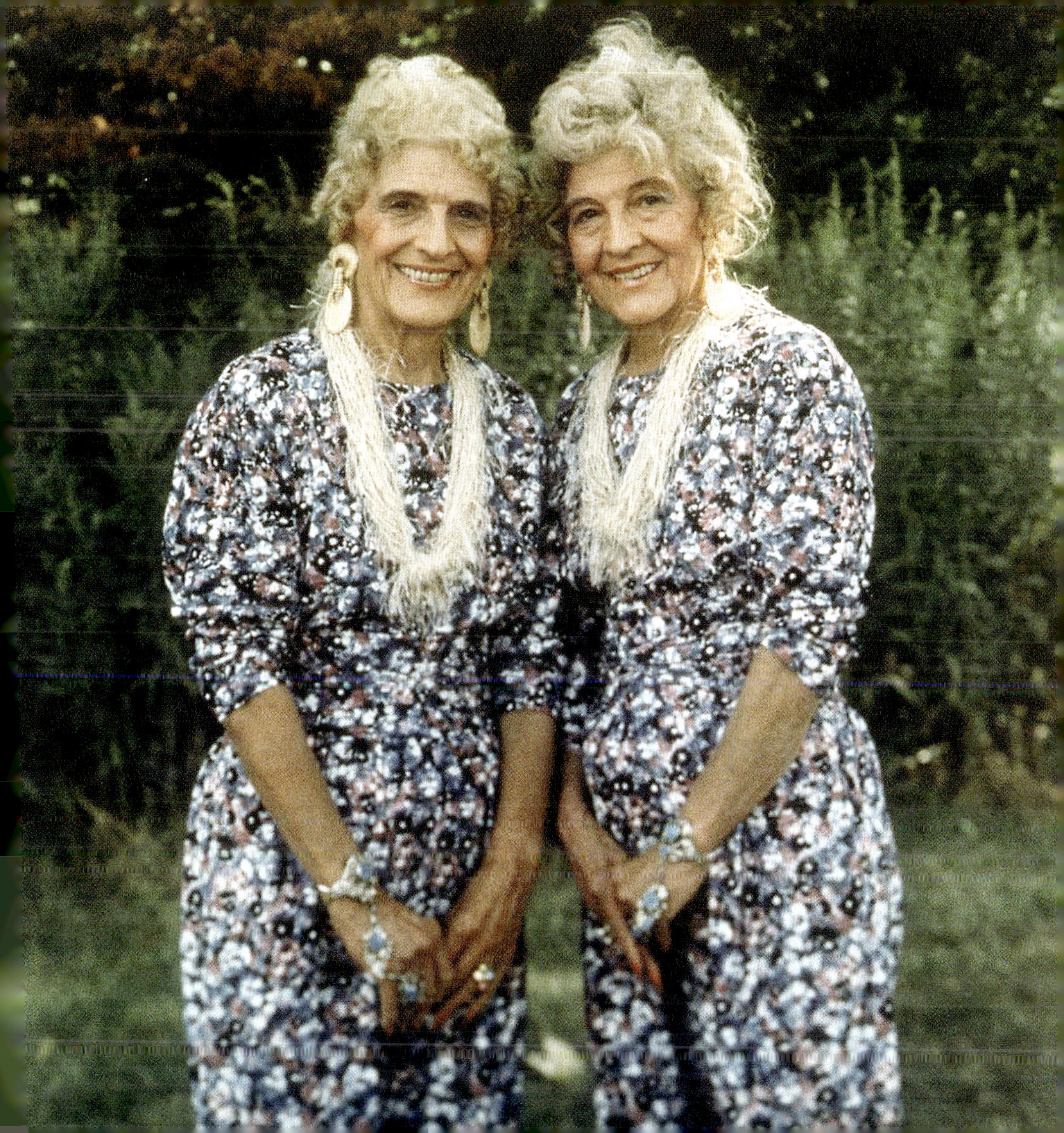

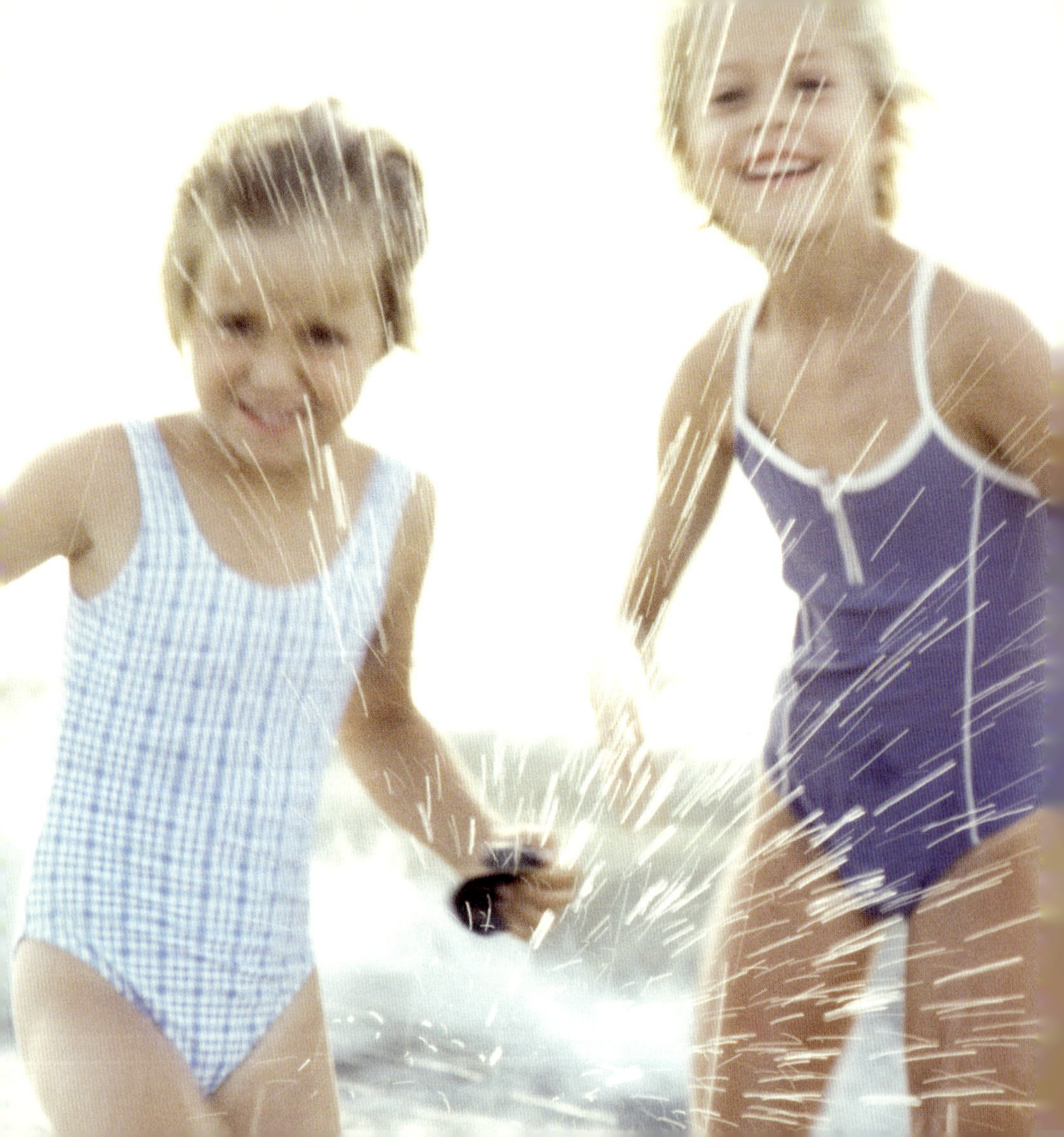

SISTERS FUNCTION AS SAFETY NETS IN

A CHAOTIC WORLD SIMPLY BY BEING

THERE FOR EACH OTHER.

—Carol Saline

We are sisters. We will always be sisters.

Our differences may never go away,

But neither, for me, will our song.

—Elizabeth Fishel

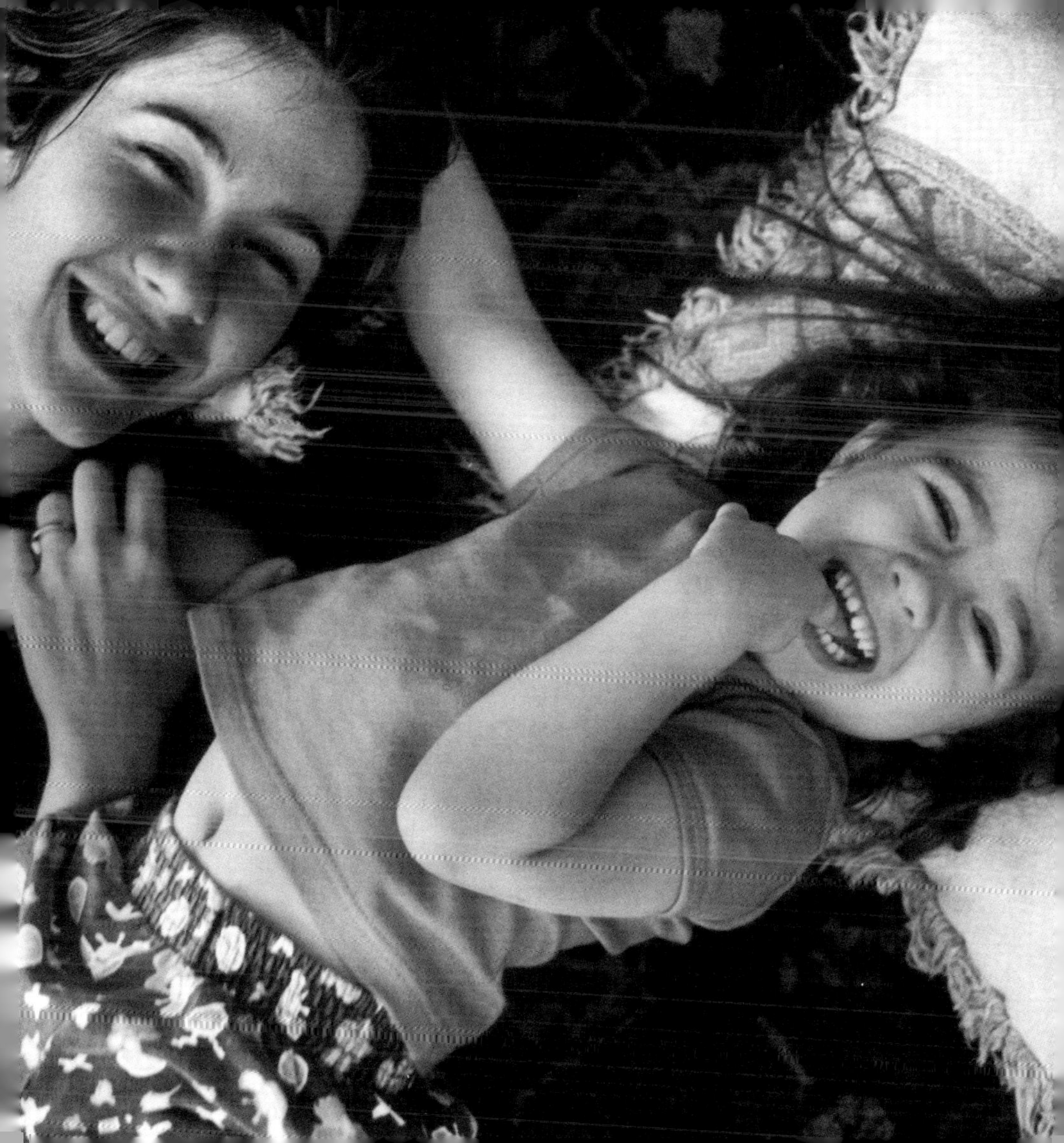

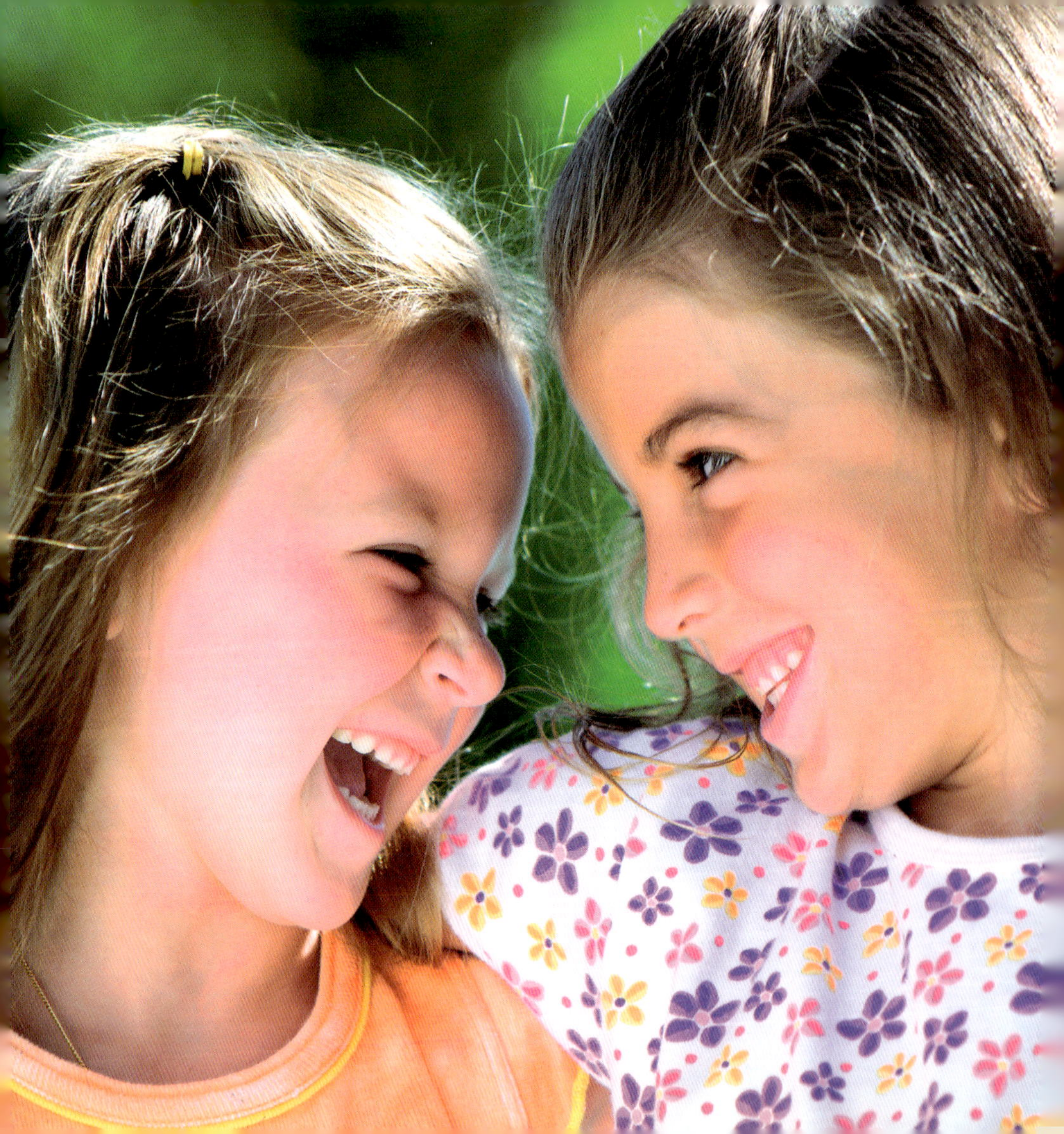

SISTERS ARE THE PEOPLE WE PRACTICE ON,

THE PEOPLE WHO TEACH US ABOUT FAIRNESS

AND COOPERATION AND KINDNESS AND CARING—

QUITE OFTEN THE HARD WAY.

—Pamela Dugdale

PHOTO CREDITS

COVER PHOTO: Ibid; P. 4: Rebecca Emery; P. 6: Andersen Ross; P. 8: Ibid; P. 10: David Troncoso; P. 12: Ibid; P. 14: ML Harris; P. 16: Gary Moss; P. 18: Plush Studios; P. 20: Andersen Ross; P. 22: Christina Kennedy; P. 24: Ibid; P. 26: Ibid; P. 28: Ibid; P. 30: Christina Kennedy; P. 32: Randy Mayor; P. 34: Andersen Ross; P. 36: Doug Crouch; P. 38: Ibid; P. 40: Ibid; P. 42: Doug Crouch; P. 44: Ibid; P. 46: Taesam Do; P. 48: Ibid; P. 50: Ben Fink; P. 52: Ibid; P. 54: trbfoto; P. 56: Frare/Davis Photography; P. 58: Ibid; P. 60: Lilly Dong; P. 62: Keith Brofsky; P. 64: trbfoto; P. 66: Peter Zander; P. 68: Ibid; P. 70: Sarah M. Golonka; P. 72: Andersen Ross; P. 74: Sarah M. Golonka; P. 76: Ibid; P. 78: Ibid; P. 80: Mark Lyon; P. 82: es; P. 85: Roger Mesquita; P. 86: SW Productions.

The beautiful photos you see throughout this book are courtesy of Jupiterimages.
For more information on the contributing photographers, visit www.jupiterimages.com.

jupiterimages.